I0027359

Also by Hazel Wagner

Power Brainstorming - Great Ideas at Lightning Speed

Speaking of Success - World Class Experts Share Their Secrets (with Ken Blanchard, Jack Canfield, and Stephen R. Covey)

Business, Brains & B.S.

A Business Mystery

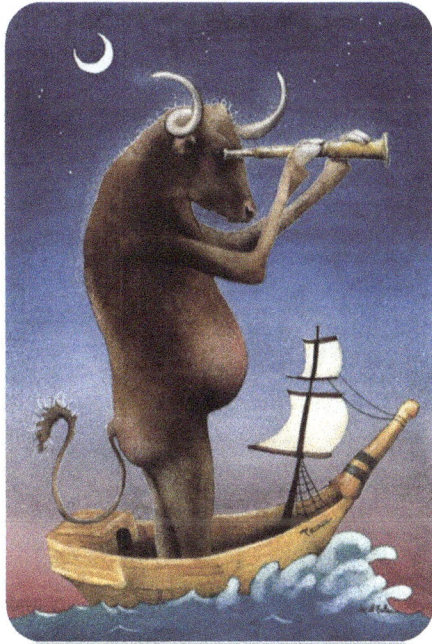

Hazel Wagner

Brainiance
Ideas · Books · Speakers

Copyright © 2014 Hazel Wagner, PhD. B9D Inc.

Part of the Brainiance Book series published by B9D, Inc.

All rights reserved for the entire book. Reproduction, scanning, uploading, distribution or any part of this work without permission of the publisher and author is unlawful in any form by any means and punishable by law.

Cover artist and several of the delightful reproductions within the book, with permission, are by Will Bullas of Carmel Valley, California. Copyright, Will Bullas.

Other artists represented with permission in this book are David Marinello and Audrey Wancket, Wancket Studios. Copyrights belong to each of the artists. Additional photographs from istock.com.

HBDI® is a registered trademark of Herrmann International and the term is used with written permission. Each of the Assessments mentioned are registered trademarks of their own company.

This publication is written and designed to provide businesses and individuals with techniques and tools to bring out and escalate natural creativity. The author and publisher do not assume any responsibility for errors, omissions, or diversity of interpretations and cannot be held liable for any business results either directly or indirectly.

The characters, companies, and situations are completely fictitious and any similarities to people or companies are purely coincidental.
ISBN-13: 978-0-9785801-2-4

TABLE OF CONTENTS

DEDICATION

This book is dedicated to my family, my husband, my children, my grandchildren, and recently, my great-grandchildren, to the sharing of their own versions of wisdom and to the wonderful power of an extended family that is held together by love and caring. Each of my children runs a company; their challenges and successes were inspiration for this book.

Pulling an All-Nighter by Will Bullas

INTRODUCTION

Wisdom is the ability to apply experience, common sense, logic, and thoughtfulness to knowledge and data. It is the ability to know which pieces of knowledge and data acquired in the past or researched on the Internet apply. It is the ability to question assumptions, one's own and others'. It is the ability to recognize and admit when you don't know an answer or aren't sure, and to be able to figure out how or where or from whom you can get answers you can trust. Wisdom is the ability to step away from a situation and look at it from different viewpoints and to know when to ask for those other viewpoints. It is the ability to look at the situation from a distance and up close. Look at the forest *and* the trees.

Some of the experience needed to develop wisdom one comes by directly. Other experience can be vicarious by reading or learning from others. This story, this business mystery, is wrapped around ideas and content intended to make you think. Accept and internalize what works for you. Be open to other viewpoints and at the same time apply your skepticism and common sense.

This book and the ideas expressed come from years of learning from and observing many others: my husband, my children and grandchildren (often wise beyond their years), my parents, my business associates (both the ones I spent years working alongside and the fleeting ones), professors, authors, and speakers who inspired me. There were people whose actions or words I immediately felt were important and others where I only later realized what I had learned. There were positive examples to emulate and negative ones to avoid.

So where does an author start and finish to thank them all? I will start with my wonderful family, an understanding husband, often pestered to read or listen so I could get immediate feedback, and three children who have taught me what it means to care about strangers as well as friends and to give more than they have available. My grandchildren taught me about the unending questions that children can ask and the natural creativity of all children that somehow gets lost over the years. My sister, whose style and path has been so different from my own has taught me how equal, and great, different can be.

My wish is for you, the reader, to come away from reading this book with some additional wisdom, to help you grow your own Business, Brains, and B.S.

1 BUSINESS SUSPENDED

SUNLIGHT SPARKLED across the gleaming marble floor. Heavy footsteps echoed down the hallway. Bursting into the office, Craig grabbed the remote control pointing it at the big screen. He scrolled through the menu to the entertainment station. Daniel stood with his mouth open, "What the?"

"Shh!" Craig put his hand out. "You've got to hear this!"

"The Movie Minute?" Daniel asked. "What is this about?"

The announcer's voice proclaimed a startling revelation by up and coming actress Melanie Myers.

"This is a miracle, I tell you, a complete miracle!" the beautiful blonde gushed into the camera.

"Why am I watching this?" Daniel fumed.

"Just wait," Craig was still gasping for breath.

"That was Melanie Myers' shocking revelation on her struggle with an aggressive autoimmune condition and receiving an experimental drug that has put her symptoms in remission. That drug is manufactured by Wilson-

Shaw Pharmaceuticals."

The remote slipped from Craig's hand, thumping on the carpet. Daniel stood frozen in the middle of his office, hands on hips, silent.

Daniel couldn't help but chuckle to himself. Both his office phone and cell were ringing non-stop, and his email box continued to ping with incoming messages. His little known company was instantly on everyone's radar. He had spent the last two hours fielding calls from the board members, other VPs in the company and the media.

Daniel called out for Brooke, serving as his assistant today since Molly didn't show up for work. It was damage control all around, and Daniel thrived in these moments.

"Yes?" Brooke appeared at the door to his office.

"Find that so-called celebrity and see if she has a publicist or whatever they have. We need to talk to her directly."

"I can find anybody," Brooke winked and turned around.

While it was too soon to release formal research findings one of the test subjects, some starlet in Hollywood, had gushed about a clinical trial she was in and how it had made her symptoms virtually disappear. How they traced it back to Wilson-Shaw was a mystery. The company wasn't prepared for the onslaught of queries, the press releases were still in draft form. Molly had been handling the media plan and now she was missing from work.

The approval from the FDA would be in jeopardy if the research were compromised, and Daniel wasn't sure what to do next.

The phone rang again – he checked the caller ID, he had to take this call.

"Hi Dad," Daniel ran his hand through his hair.

"Danny, what the hell is going on? Have you seen the stock futures?"

"Not in the last hour, but when I saw them they were on the way up. I'm not sure what we can do; we could end up incredibly rich or flat broke by the end of the day."

"I'll tell you what to do," his dad barked. "You'll…won't take this…reposition…" The line went dead.

Daniel let out a long breath and tossed his cell phone on the desk. This time he wasn't too upset about a dropped call. He knew exactly what his dad was saying, it was always the same. He wished they had the luxury or monotony of everything happening the same way each time. Business, heck, life itself constantly changes and evolves, problems look different all the time, yet his dad's mantra was "We've always done it this way. It worked before, and it will work again."

He turned toward the window and looked out over the grounds. Wilson-Shaw wasn't a major player in the pharmaceutical industry…yet. The big names had huge campuses with acres of buildings housing labs, marketing departments, and shiny executive offices. Wilson-Shaw only had a few products. This new formula, known as RQ246, was their first shot at the big time. In taking over the reins of the company, Daniel convinced the board of directors to approve a huge capital investment in bringing several new scientists on board, solely with the mission to develop a new drug to treat skin outbreaks from autoimmune diseases. Over the past four years, the lab had been working double shifts on the new formulation. The trials were the last major component of the launch process. They were only weeks away from announcing the results and, Daniel was convinced, FDA approval.

He remembered sharing his ideas with Molly, his assistant for nearly eight years. He moved her into the executive position when he was named CEO. She understood his quirks, covered for him when he needed to hide out to get some work done, and never balked at staying late or coming in on the weekends to help finish up a project. They worked well together; she was always studying new ways to look at things. She had a fascination with how the brain worked and how using Brainiant techniques businesses could be more creative and successful. She fed him ideas, which he presented, usually to the extreme approval of the board and his underlings. As a working partnership it was clear that they were well matched.

It wasn't like her to miss a day of work, let alone be so out of touch. He thought he remembered something about family visiting but he never approved any time off. Maybe he did approve it, there had been so much going on, he couldn't be sure.

One of Daniel's biggest peeves was the 'That's the way we've always done it' chorus he heard from his dad, Harold Wilson Shaw, and the board. Harold, never Harry, had been a driving force in growing the company from a small custom formulary service to a certified manufacturer. Harold was always making knee-jerk reactions and quick decisions. He would push his people to act, saying that any decision was better than no decision. Yet the organic matter would really hit the fan when they went wrong.

Daniel preferred to think things through carefully and gather as many opinions as possible before making a decision, which made Harold even more impatient. Daniel wouldn't be where he was today if it weren't for Harold just deciding one day that he had enough and was ready to retire. That lasted one winter, which his parents spent enjoying the warmth of sunny Florida. His mother told Daniel that it was the long awaited second honeymoon that she had hoped for. Then, she died suddenly of a heart attack and his dad was adrift. After a few weeks of aimless wandering through shopping malls and hanging around the library, Daniel asked him to come back to Wilson-Shaw and work as a consultant.

As the new leader, Daniel worked to foster a more creative environment, hiring experts to lead workshops on creativity and thinking styles so everyone had the confidence and opportunity to suggest improvements or pitch ideas for new products. He still wondered how he was able to convince the board to approve the research funding. But that was three years ago and here they were, so close to completing one of his visions,. not to mention the thousands of lives improved by the new drug. He was still staring out the window when he heard a knock, he turned to see Brad, the CFO.

"Tell me this isn't happening," Brad implored.

"I wish I could. I don't know for sure what has happened," Daniel answered. "All I know is that Wilson-Shaw was mentioned on some Hollywood report this morning, this two-bit actress made a startling confession about how lucky she was to be in a clinical trial."

"How would anyone know the company? This puts us in great jeopardy, it could set us back years," Brad's voice was breaking.

"I have no clue." Daniel turned back toward the window. He was antsy and needed to get out of the office. "Come on, let's go to the club, I need to run some of this off and clear my head."

Brad shook his head. "Can't, I've got a ton of emails to answer and we need to start planning a strategy to deal with a value increase that we've never expected. Running right now won't cut it for me. And why the hell is Molly out today?"

Daniel shrugged and walked out, leaving Brad standing in his office. Brad was a bit nervous for his taste anyway. He looked around for Brooke, no she was missing. Without breaking stride, he pulled out his cell phone and sent her a text message: *Out for a run, call if you need me.*

He rounded the corner to see the VP of Sales at the elevator. He didn't have the time or the patience for a chat, so he ducked into the stairwell and bounded down the stairs. By the time he was at the bottom, his heart was pounding so hard he could hear it.

Once he got to the club, the tightness in his chest alarmed him. He realized he hadn't been breathing. He scanned his pass at the desk and rushed into the locker room. He was beginning to feel light headed. He sat on the bench in front of it his locker, dropping his head into his hands. He just needed to slow down for a minute, take a deep breath and calm down.

A slamming locker nearby shattered the quiet. He turned to see one of the guys that played in the pick-up basketball games.

"How's it going?"

"Busy day, just need a run to clear my head," Daniel replied.

"I hear you. We're playing pick-up games at seven tomorrow morning. We haven't seen you in a while. You ought to join us."

"I'll keep that in mind, thanks." He changed into his gear and headed for the cardio room. Daniel felt his only sense of control was when he could go for a run. He liked it upstairs where the high-end treadmills faced out along a bank of floor to ceiling windows that looked out over the busy street below. The treadmills were sleek and silent, he could let himself get hypnotized by the whispering belt and lose himself for a while. Watching the people below, he would imagine their lives, their problems, and wonder if they would trade places.

He had a lot to sort out. How to respond to the slip in protocol, what he would tell the board, and whatever positive spin they could eke out of the whole mess. One positive aspect was this actress claiming RQ246 had cleared all her symptoms. If indeed she had the real drug and not the placebo, then that meant success for the drug and the company. But how did she even know what the drug was or who the manufacturer was? How did their little company, in the middle of nowhere end up as part of Hollywood gossip?

He jabbed at the incline button and cranked up the speed. Thinking back over the past several months, he tried to pinpoint any time he might have let word of the drug trial slip. He had attended several conventions, and could only remember making vague references while enjoying a round of golf with his good friend Gary Brownlee and a couple of guys from Manning Solutions. They manufactured hospital beds and accessories, so it seemed odd that they would repeat anything he said. He knew Gary would keep anything he said in confidence. Daniel was certain he hadn't mentioned specifics. Besides, they had already made it through Phase 2 trials. It was nearly a sure thing.

He continued to retrace his conversations, everyone involved had signed non-disclosure agreements within the company. The outside legal counsel was also sworn to secrecy. Daniel knew he hadn't compromised the company. He increased the incline one more notch.

Running a pharmaceutical company was pretty cut and dried, the standards were in place for a reason, to reduce risk and ultimately protect potential users. Daniel felt that creativity and innovation was just as important, it would lead to new research and drugs. He could understand why his dad was hesitant to break out and go into unchartered territory. But Daniel also knew that the complications from autoimmune diseases hit too close to home. He remembered his Aunt Debbie, when struck down with the disease, went from vivacious and active, to shut in and fearful of being out in public.

He knew if he could just get RQ246 through, it would be an entire shift for the company. They would be a big player, not just some generic manufacturer taking on runs for other companies. It would demonstrate that he was a true leader, not just the family heir. He needed this to work, his marriage was about to disintegrate while he was immersed in taking over the reins of the company. He figured that was just part of the process.

He had made a feeble attempt to go to marriage counseling, but he was already swamped with taking on the leadership position at Wilson-Shaw. The board of directions required him to complete several professional development workshops before announcing him as CEO.

One of the workshops focused on diversity of thinking styles. It helped him realize the differences between him and his father; such as seeing ideas, versus hearing or feeling them. He was excited about incorporating different thinkers into this type of team work. But Harold swiftly shot down the idea. Understanding that feeling ideas was acceptable gave Daniel a sense of relief. He often would feel the physical anxiety build up to the point he couldn't hold still. He *needed* to go run or shoot baskets or play a game of racquetball. Afterward, he had a renewed sense of calm and focus.

During the workshop, the facilitator discussed various tests to determine thinking styles. While he was intrigued, Daniel didn't do it then, he was just happy to have the validation that it was ok to feel ideas. Many times Daniel would map out the workflow and walk himself through the steps. Even though graphic artists were handling all the design of the marketing material, Daniel wanted to handle all the brochures and put himself in the place of a physician or one of the marketing representatives. He didn't think that it was unreasonable.

He remembered when he and his wife CeeCee went shopping for a new sofa. She was going to go pick something out since Daniel was so busy, but he made time to be there. How could someone buy a sofa without actually sitting on it or feeling it? He didn't like that rough Berber upholstery, yet CeeCee loved how it looked. He preferred the buttery soft feel of leather; she loathed the look of leather. It seemed to be so insignificant at the time, but then learning about his feeling style, he could understand where the conflict lay. He was all about the feel, she was all about the look. Finally, they compromised and reached an agreement. Ironically, he hasn't spent much time sitting on the new couch.

Any time things got tough at the office, Daniel fought within himself, one minute doubting his ability to run the company then the next, wanting to prove to Harold he could do the job and do it well. He struggled with the fine line between delegating the top level responsibilities and giving away control. While he appreciated his dad's experiences in running the company, it seemed so much more complicated now than when Harold took over from his father, Grandpa Wilson. Under his dad's wing, the company went public and there had been some power struggles with the first board of directors.

Daniel campaigned heavily to bring on other employees to strengthen the company, he needed to make sure the skill sets, attitudes, loyalty, energy and integrity matched his expectations and they had the capability and desire to learn. He expanded the job search criteria to invite foreign researchers and chemists on work study visas. Going global would mean bringing the globe to Wilson-Shaw.

Two Chinese graduate students had been great contributors to the research on RQ246. Harold had opposed the idea, but after a few months, became more comfortable with it. That led to adding another work-study research assistant from India. While Daniel wasn't scientific, he did appreciate the interaction and input they demonstrated in work group meetings.

Everything had been moving along smoothly through the development and research trials. Now, the sudden media leak has thrown everything off balance.

Bonus Stuff: Each thinking style[1] views change differently and deals with it in its own way.
- A—Tends to be pragmatic; what are the facts? It needs to get done, let's do it quickly and efficiently.
- B—Needs the planning and steps to be taken before getting started.
- C—Wants stability, worries about who will be impacted, and how to keep everything running smoothly with the least upset.
- D—Looks at change as fun and empowering, focuses on the big picture.

---

[1] HBDI®, DISC, MBTI®, and Mindex® are 3 types of assessments. For more information on any of them, contact Hazel Wagner.

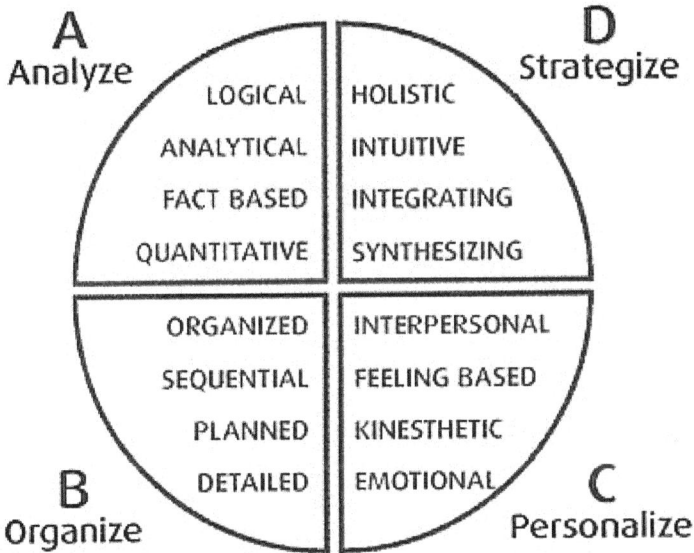

A
Analyze

D
Strategize

LOGICAL	HOLISTIC
ANALYTICAL	INTUITIVE
FACT BASED	INTEGRATING
QUANTITATIVE	SYNTHESIZING
ORGANIZED	INTERPERSONAL
SEQUENTIAL	FEELING BASED
PLANNED	KINESTHETIC
DETAILED	EMOTIONAL

B
Organize

C
Personalize

For change to be effective in an organization, all four styles need to be addressed. Most of all, attention should be paid to the attitudes toward each other as the change proceeds. Each person needs to understand how and why they contribute to the change process, and ultimately, the success of the organization. Change is less about the physical things that transform and more about employees' views and sense of worth in the process. Once employees see how things can get better they take a more active role in making sure the change is successful. They look for ways to make it work.

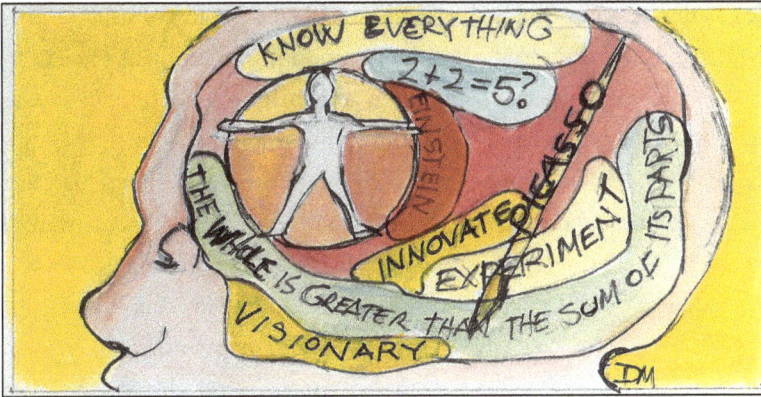

Know Everything by David Marinello

2 BACK SPIN

MOLLY WOKE slowly to the sound of the pounding surf outside her door. The sun was already so bright that it was slicing its way into the dark room around the edges of the ratty drapes. "I really did do this," she said to herself.

She fumbled for her phone on the nightstand. There were several texts, some from Brooke, two from Brad, yet none from her boss. Brooke's texts were all questions; where were the press release drafts, did she have PTO approved, and had she heard about Melanie Meyers?

She laid back and listened to the surf and her growling stomach. She needed this break, just not under the circumstances. Just a few days away from work, Daniel's restless energy, the tension between him and Harold. Harold was constantly calling Molly when he disagreed with Daniel's decisions. There were five voicemails from Harold; she was sure they were all tirades against Daniel. She had no energy to deal with any of it.

The cheap hotel along route 234 was a random, spontaneous choice. At least it had a coffee maker, which sputtered and splattered out hot liquid with an ebony tinge. She took a sip. Slightly bitter, but tolerable.

She pushed back the drapes and looked out at the water. It was high tide and the waves had moved much closer to the patio. An elderly couple walked by in lock step. The woman was waving her hands and chattering away while the gentlemen nodded and kept the pace. Molly wondered what it would be like to have someone special to walk the beach with every morning. A sweet little house, a family, something a little slower paced. Yet all she was ever told was that she was such a brainy girl who didn't need to get bogged down with a normal life. She enjoyed brain teasers and learning how to think more critically and creatively. Many times she gave Daniel new ideas or perspectives, which nearly always led to that aha moment for him.

She picked up her journal and walked out onto the little patio outside her door. Folded inside was a magazine article that she had torn out while waiting at the dentist a few weeks ago. She smoothed out the pages and began to read.

"Your Brain and how it fools you:

You absolutely can learn to use your brain better, would you like to be able to do that?

How would you like to be better at problem solving, critical thinking skills, creative ideas while being recognized as a better listener and communicator?

As a math teacher, even if the answer was incorrect, I'd ask, 'How did you get that answer?' A correct method was just as important, in fact more important, than the correct answer because only a correct method gave the student the ability to apply the method of thinking to new situations. Maybe it was right in certain situations or maybe there was flawed thinking that they would see in trying to explain how they had gotten the answer.

Now relate that to business. Innovation requires creativity which requires diversity of thinking and thinking styles. If we all looked at every problem and situation the same way we'd never come up with any differentiated products or services.

How does a company foster an environment where diversity thinking, option thinking and creativity in problem solving is normal operating procedure? These companies recognize it is best to consider as many options as possible before making decisions. They also encourage everyone, from any level not just management, to contribute ideas on how to make improvements, *imagine new products or services, or new ways to accomplish something."*

Molly shook her head. Even though Harold frequently bent her ear about Daniel, she couldn't get through to him that everyone's ideas were valid. Maybe she contributed to the tension between father and son. Daniel wanted to collect ideas and opinions, while Harold made a decision and wouldn't budge unless there were mountains of data and even then, he was reluctant.

"More ideas allow for more good ideas to flow to the top. But just idea generation won't run a business. The key is to look for and be open to new ideas while applying logic, wisdom, and experience. Large numbers of options does not mean analysis paralysis. This is a quick and useful method for looking at many sides of a situation and be sure it is understood before jumping to a conclusion.

It is often said that there isn't really anything new, only new combinations and permutations. The ability to apply new combinations and permutations will accelerate your idea generation and bring out the creativity in your brain and your team.

Every company can nurture creativity by allowing and encouraging all ideas sometimes including ideas that fail, before employees are willing to shine a light on their ideas. Too often they are afraid to mention their idea and it is the company's loss. Either the idea is good and can be developed further and exploited or it is not and can be mined for what would make it into a good idea or for parts and pieces that can accelerate good ideas. Some of the best ideas come from putting two or three independent ideas together."

Molly was startled by the squawking of several gulls who were fighting over a small crab at the water's edge. She stared out over the vast, unending ocean. There wasn't a cloud in the sky. She thought about the line, "allowing bad ideas and ideas that fail." In Harold's day, a bad idea meant a pink slip. Daniel would say he was all for all ideas, good and bad, but under Harold's shadow, he often lost courage. Molly kept a notebook of all the 'bad' ideas that Daniel wanted to revisit. Many times they would discuss them. She would help him sort it out. While he usually recognized her contribution, sometimes he presented an idea as his own which was frustrating. Yet he was faithful to her as a boss, she had proved her value and he relied on her heavily.

"There are many ways for this to happen naturally. Get people talking! The water cooler is still a powerful business strategy. Associates that don't sit next to each other can chat about what they are working on or a decision they have to make.

Design your workspaces to encourage collaboration and chance meetings. Hopefully you still have a water cooler of some sort. Many companies have kitchens or snack areas with tables and chairs. Incorporate picnic tables outside where not just lunch but meetings can be held in nice weather.

Apple arranged their building so even the rest rooms were a place for impromptu talks. The only problem with those is that they leave out either men or women. When I worked for a major tech corporation there were very few women on the sales management team. Men would come out of the rest room talking and laughing as if they had shared something important. When asked, females got a surprised look and the usual comment, 'Oh, nothing.'

Coffee, juice, water, a place to sit in the sun or shade are all great encouragers of idea exploration."

Molly smiled to herself. She had already had that idea at Wilson-Shaw. There was a sleek new cafeteria in the basement, but it felt like they were hiding out in a bunker. There was no sunlight, no windows. Daniel didn't see the value of smaller gathering areas at first, but she persisted. Small kitchenettes and lounge areas weren't time wasters, they were demonstrating that they helped people talk.

A sidebar in the article caught her eye. "*There are also many ways to discover what happens when two or more disparate ideas get juxtaposed by using Power Brainstorming techniques. Pick two words at random from a dictionary or magazine and ask everyone to write three ways those words connect. Share the results and build from there.*

You can even push the direction a bit by choosing a noun from one of the project descriptions and a verb from the other. Put them together in 10 different sentences."

Molly could hear her cell phone buzzing inside the room. She leaned back and closed her eyes. She wasn't ready to answer it or let anyone know where she was.

B onus Stuff: Resistance or complaints about brainstorming are often the result of misunderstanding the true spirit of brainstorming. Trying to formalize it or force it kills the spirit.

Brainstorming works best when groups are kept small. A group of three to five works well since it is small enough that no one feels like they can sit back and just watch. However, the group should be large enough to include diversity of thinking styles.

Invite at least one person who doesn't work with your group on a regular basis. Fresh eyes and ears bring in new perspectives. Someone to whom the subject is new will ask interesting and naive questions that are needed to bring about new directions in thinking.

Some truths about brainstorming:

1. Quantity is more important than quality, especially in the beginning.
2. First old ideas will emerge, then more creative ones, ideas that build on old ideas, then finally breakthrough ideas will surface.
3. Starting with brainstorming questions instead of answers will improve the brainstorming productivity.
4. Use every question or class of questions as the jumping off point, or center of a mind-map.
5. To increase everyone's brain activity, be sure all four thinking style quadrants are being tickled.

A Classic by David Marinello

3 BLIND SIGHT

AS HE PULLED into the driveway, Daniel realized he didn't remember any of the drive home. His phone had been ringing non-stop all day, but he couldn't remember if he was talking to someone while he drove. With the whirlwind of attention around the leak, his day had been nonstop. He was screening applicants for the VP of Development position and reviewing the annual report before it went to print. Every day it seemed as if there were a new urgent project.

The open position was critical though, Fred Hirsch, the former VP, had died while hiking Grand Canyon. It was his first vacation in over two years.

He had been a leader in bringing QR246 to trial. His death sent a shock wave throughout the company. The only good result from his death was the revamping of the personal time off policy—employees were now docked if they did not take some time off. The company had an exclusive arrangement with a local travel agent for discounted services, and a recreation and wellness specialist had been brought onboard to coordinate company outings, off site work retreats and intermural sports.

Daniel was proud of those changes, and he was beginning to see people embracing a more active lifestyle. However, Harold wasn't sold on the idea. "It's like paying them to goof off," he barked one day. Daniel just shrugged it off, he knew how much relief running gave him. He felt more energized and clear-headed after a run. It was a slow culture shift within the company, but it was beginning to produce benefits.

With a long deep breath, Daniel turned off the car and leaned his head back against the headrest. The garage light clicked off and he felt the darkness and silence wrap around him.

"Dan?"

He looked up to see CeeCee's hand on his shoulder.

"Honey, are you ok? You fell asleep in here," she asked.

"Wow, I just put my head back for a second. I'm ok, just a hell of a day." Daniel unbuckled the seat belt and began to get out of the car. "A hell of a day."

"Why don't you come in and sit down for a minute, I'll get you a drink and you can fill me in. I have a feeling the Hollywood buzz has to do with some of it," she said.

"You don't know the half of it," Daniel began. "My phone never stopped today. Most of it was flak from the board of directors, demanding to know how word got leaked. CeeCee, I don't know how that got out, and it certainly doesn't help us make it through the trial unbiased. On the flip side, if she really did receive the drug, it's great for us."

CeeCee dropped two ice cubes in a tumbler and retrieved the honey infused bourbon from under the sink. The amber liquid splashed over the cubes, releasing a warm, sweet fragrance. Daniel kicked off his shoes and loosened his tie as she carried the glass over to him.

"None for you?" he asked.

"Not right now, I have a call with a client on the west coast in a few minutes."

Daniel looked puzzled. "West coast? You're not the leak, are you?"

"Are you kidding me? You're sounding crazy again. This is the jewelry designer from Chicago. She is spending a couple months in California, so we are just adjusting the schedule."

The two locked eyes. Daniel knew he didn't pay much attention to his wife's business as a copywriter. She told him things she was working on from time to time, but he usually tuned it out. CeeCee was always asking him about his work and at times it seemed like too many questions. When they first met, he was smitten with her inquisitive nature, always digging for more information. Lately, all her questions irritated him.

He was so excited for her when she snagged her first big client, an eco-friendly packaging company. She became busier with her work and he moved into the CEO position. That was when the two really started living separate lives.

"Dan, I don't like the way you're looking at me. Why in the world would I say anything to anyone about the drug trial? I just know snippets of what you are working on and only what you've told me about the trial process. Do you honestly suspect me of telling corporate secrets?"

Did he? Daniel took a long, slow sip of the bourbon and closed his eyes.

"Cee, I don't know what I'm thinking. I am utterly exhausted, I'm going to bed." Daniel struggled off the couch and tipped the tumbler up as the final drops ran onto his tongue. He set it on the side table. "Night."

Around 2 a.m. the neighbor's dog began to bark. Daniel woke up to find CeeCee's side of the bed untouched. It wasn't unusual anymore, she had been sleeping on the futon in her office more than in the bedroom. Daniel plumped his pillow, turned on the CD of ocean sounds and tried to go back to sleep. His mind refused to stop. Thoughts were racing. Who could he trust? Who could have possibly leaked the info about the drug? Who was this actress anyway? How did she find out about the trial? Will they make it to market? Should he even be in charge of the company?

He sat upright and turned on the light. The dog had stopped barking, but he could hear a car running outside. He suddenly turned the light off and peered through the blinds. He fumbled for his phone and pulled up the home alarm app. The alarm was on. The dog barked again. The car engine revved and he could see the lights heading down the street. Daniel let out a deep sigh and turned on the light again. He grabbed the pen and pad by the bed and started to make a list:

The leak

Annual Report

Drug trial

College fund for Katie

Oil change

Molly's mysterious absence

Left knee is sore again

He looked back over the list. That should be enough. He turned off the light, rolled over and fell asleep.

The light through the bedroom window was brighter than he thought it should be at this hour. He looked at the clock, 7:15; damn, overslept. He bolted out of bed and went straight to the shower. Damn CeeCee, he thought. Why didn't she wake me up?

After the shower he followed the aroma of fresh brewed coffee to the kitchen only to find a note from CeeCee, *Took Katie to early orthodontist appt.*

Even though CeeCee and their daughter were already gone, he looked for evidence of their son, Josh. Other than an empty cereal box on the counter, Daniel wasn't sure if he had left for school. Since the kids were in high school, they were usually both gone from before breakfast to late at night thanks to sports and part time jobs. Daniel wanted them to understand what it was like to work their way through college, just as he had. Katie was headed off to college in the fall, she just needed to finalize her decision.

Daniel realized he had what everyone longed for; an impressive salary, a powerful position, a beautiful wife and healthy children, nice cars, country club membership, and a home that would be showcased in any magazine. Yet, he still doubted his ability to stay on top of things at work, or perform as CEO. Even when he felt like he had work well in hand, he realized that his home life was a mess. His kids were independent, he and CeeCee didn't spend much time together.

His cell phone broke the silence.

"Good morning Dad."

"Danny, where the hell are you? We've got a mess here," Harold barked.

"I'm on my way, what's going on?"

"Wilson-Shaw was mentioned on the stock report this morning, and the shares shot up. So far, there are online two articles stating we purposely leaked the drug trial."

"Doesn't sound like much of a mess," Daniel chuckled.

"Don't you understand? If the FDA thinks we purposely leaked the drug trial just to raise stock prices they can stop the approval. We'll be dead in the water. We'll have the OCI all over us."

Daniel couldn't have picked a worse time to drive to the office. He got caught behind a school bus, then the garbage truck, and finally had to wait for a freight train to cross. Each time he came to a stop he checked his phone for emails. They were pouring in fast. He couldn't do anything to answer them now, his mind was still on his Dad's comment about the OCI. In the wake of the generic drug scandal in 1991, the Commissioner of Food and Drugs established the Office of Criminal Investigations (OCI) within the Food and Drug Administration. Daniel relied on the legal team to keep all that in check. But he couldn't help wondering, how do you know what you don't know? Were they heading off in their own direction without keeping Wilson-Shaw's mission in mind? Who was minding the store? The feelings of inadequacy were closing in. He hadn't even made it to the office yet and wanted to run again.

His thoughts were interrupted by the buzz of his phone—CeeCee—for a second he considered letting it go to voicemail. At the last ring he hit the on button on his hands free device.

"Good morning sunshine."

"It is a good morning," CeeCee's voice was clear and bright. "I've just signed Art Lauder, a year contract! I've been chasing him for over 18 months."

"That's great honey," Daniel's voice began to crack. He was finding it difficult to be enthusiastic. This meant CeeCee would be traveling more. He wasn't sure he liked that idea.

"You're not too excited, I can hear it in your voice," she replied.

"I'm happy for you, it's great. It's just that from what you told me, you'll be away more."

"And you'll miss me?" CeeCee smirked.

"I think it will make what is difficult even more so. The kids will never see us." Daniel said.

"The kids are already very self-sufficient, and as for us, maybe more absence will help. You know, absence makes the heart grow fonder? Besides, you might as well just set up a cot at the company until this whole drug trial is over."

"Yeah, I overslept this morning and Dad has already been on my case about it. I think this is going to be a very bumpy ride."

"Well, I'll let you concentrate on the road, I just wanted to check in and tell you the good news. Catch ya later." The line went dead. She had already hung up.

"Well, good bye to you too," Daniel's voice trailed off. He wondered what she was really up to. The contract meant she would be flying to the west coast on a regular basis. He tried to calm his thoughts, surely she wasn't the leak. Would she be out in California tossing around privileged info? She understood the gravity of the trial process. I'm just being paranoid, he thought to himself.

He was nearly to the office when his phone rang again.

"Danny boy!" Gary's voice boomed.

Daniel smiled and relaxed. "Hey big guy, what's the good word?"

"You tell me, Wilson-Shaw is all over the news. What are you doing? Is this a good thing or bad thing, the whole Hollywood business?" Gary asked.

"Too soon to tell. The stocks are shooting up, but that could come back to smack us in the ass if it looks like we manipulated the leak in order to be more valuable. We didn't have any plan in place for this, who knew something like this would happen? We've done the trial by the book. It's anybody's guess at this point," Daniel sighed heavily.

"Brother, you are sounding stressed, so I've got just the thing for you. Skybox tickets for the game tomorrow afternoon."

"Thanks, but I really can't, or shouldn't. Not with all this going on," Daniel replied.

"On the contrary – get out, look confident and keep those media hounds busy. Besides, there are some people that you may want to meet. I think it would do you a world of good. I'll send a car for you around noon.

I'm hanging up and will turn off my phone so you can't refuse," Gary chuckled.

"I doubt this is a good thing, but I'll be there. Looking forward to it."

Bonus Stuff: Your brain makes assumptions all the time. Yes you may be remembering the warning about ASSUME as what an assumption does to you and me, but that doesn't stop our brain for continuing on that path. Our brain has learned that without assumptions we would have to wait until we collected 100% of applicable data for every decision and that isn't feasible. What is feasible is recognizing whenever we make an assumption so we can admit and be ready to reconsider if new information becomes available.

An assumption is a statement made without proof or evidence. Sometimes the evidence exists and just wasn't mentioned. Sometimes the statement is purely someone's opinion. Think of it this way:

A continuum, a line from opinion to fact.

Opinion ←------------------------→ Fact

An assumption can fit anywhere along the line. If you are going to be making important decisions about your business and your life, you need to know and monitor how facts, credibility, and evidence support the statement.

First we must recognize assumptions, ours and others', so that we search out or request evidence. Ask, "How do you know that?" Or "How do I know that?

Hoos on First by Will Bullas

4 BOX SEAT

By the time Daniel slid into the back seat of the limo he felt he had endured beatings for the last 24 hours. Everyone at Wilson-Shaw had been in panic response, and he realized that some time away from the chaos would do him good.

Gary had a way of helping him see the lighter side of things. He was always into the latest brain techniques and technology. Even as kids, Gary was the one reading *Omni Magazine* while the rest of the kids collected comic books. Daniel couldn't disagree with the result, Gary had started several successful businesses. While his Dad scoffed at the idea, "Gary can't stay in one place very long, what's the purpose of starting a company if you're just going to sell it off?" Daniel envied Gary's entrepreneurial bent.

It also made him one of the most connected people Daniel knew. No matter where he went with Gary, they would run into someone that knew him.

Gary had taught him the parking lot technique; writing down everything that was cluttering your mind and mentally parking it until you could concentrate on it later. Before learning that, Daniel would lay awake at night and race through everything he needed to do and had done that day. As things at work escalated, so did the mind chatter.

Daniel was looking forward to the game, but more importantly, the time to bounce some ideas off Gary and see what he was up to.

The car stopped in front of the stadium. The chauffer handed him an envelope with his ticket. "Mr. Brownlee will meet you in the skybox. Enjoy the game, I hear it's supposed to be a close one," he smiled and handed Daniel his card. I'll be here after the game, if you decide to leave earlier, just call this number."

Daniel nodded, "Thank you."

The crowd around the stadium was buzzing. Daniel walked through a cluster of giggling high school girls, wondering for a moment where his own kids were. Are they in school today or skipping? He knew Katie was not one to skip—she was laser focused on her GPA and getting accepted into a top school. Josh was more like him, always looking for any excuse to escape. It was difficult to stay in one place and concentrate for long. He could see how that would serve him well at some point, it just didn't fit into the public school model very well. It was also a bone of contention between him and CeeCee. She felt Josh wasn't taking things seriously, Daniel viewed it as being bored with the slow pace of school. Josh was a pretty intelligent kid, he just showed it differently than Katie.

He approached the gate and presented the envelope. "Right this way sir," the attendant scanned the ticket and pointed to the elevator. "Enjoy the game."

Daniel couldn't help but smile to himself about the star treatment. It still seemed new to him, the limos, the prime seats. Gary had included him on many occasions like this, even when Daniel was starting out at the company. He had to prove himself and work his way up, just as his Dad did when Grandpa Wilson ran the company. It was a little more difficult once they went public, the board of directors seemed to go harder on the original family members. He supposed that was a good thing for the stockholders.

He rode the elevator alone to the sky deck level. He loved going to the games, but as much fun as it was to hang out in the prime seats, he was away from the sounds and intimacy of the game. These first warm days of spring were tantalizing, he couldn't wait to get outside to run instead of using the treadmill at the gym.

The elevator opened and another attendant greeted him. Daniel handed him the envelope, "The suite is ahead, second door on the right," the attendant motioned with a smile.

"Danny boy!" Gary's voice filled the corridor. The two met with a hearty handshake, then Gary opened his arms and engulfed Daniel in a huge bear hug.

"Good to see you," Daniel said.

"You too—we've been out of sync for a while. I've been wrapping up a new IPO, but once I saw Wilson-Shaw on the news I knew I needed to get you out for some fresh air and baseball."

"Not too much fresh air in the box," Daniel joked.

"There is today, we've opened the windows, it's perfect." Gary led Daniel to the door.

Inside the suite were two other men, Gary introduced them as Frank and Greg, both with an internet company. Daniel didn't like the looks of Greg, something about him rubbed him the wrong way immediately. Gary picked up on it and pulled Daniel aside.

"Let's get you a drink, what would you like?" he asked. He leaned in closer and whispered. "What's with the cold shoulder? You don't seem to like that guy."

Daniel turned toward the coffee pot and kept his head down while he poured a cup. "Don't know, just a weird gut reaction. Maybe he reminds me of someone. No worries, we'll enjoy the game."

No sooner than he poured his cup of coffee Greg approached him. "Daniel, tell me about your company. I believe I've heard of Wilson-Shaw, just in the last few days I think."

"The whole world has," Daniel replied. "Seems we had a bit of notoriety by some actress in Hollywood. She named our drug which is in the FDA approval process. It's not supposed to be public until it is approved. We're on top of it though." Daniel forced a smile.

"Well, any publicity is good publicity," Greg laughed and slapped Daniel's shoulder, nearly spilling his coffee. What a dick, he thought, I can't believe Gary brought him along. He looked around for Gary, who had disappeared. He walked over to the window and looked down at the batters practicing on the lush green field.

"Here's the rest of our party," Gary's voice boomed. Daniel turned to see four other men enter the suite. Behind them was a server with a tray of appetizers.

"Gentlemen, meet Brad, Clint, Shane and Travis. They are all with Green Planet, a high tech recycling company."

Daniel began to relax, he shook hands with the new guys and felt better that he wouldn't be stuck with Greg talking to him all day. Even though he needed to represent the company, Daniel felt more comfortable hanging back and observing others and their conversations. He could play the part when he needed to, making small talk and introducing himself. He was well armed with some open ended questions, and usually, other high level executives would take the opportunity and run with it. That left him listening, which he was more comfortable doing.

Soon after the introductions, the small talk turned to the game, early team standings and the weather. The men stood at the window and watched the action below.

The pre-game activities began and soon everyone was asked to stand for the National Anthem. Gary removed his cap and placed it over his heart. He caught a glimpse of Daniel looking at him and winked. One thing Daniel admired about Gary was his patriotism. He wished more people were like that.

Daniel looked down at the gigantic American flag unfurled on the field. He had wanted to enlist instead of attending college, but Harold and Grandpa Wilson wouldn't hear of it. They had determined his succession as head of Wilson-Shaw. It was the first of many times that Daniel didn't fight the family.

As the music ended, the stadium erupted into cheers. He felt the excitement and couldn't wait for the game to get started. He leaned back in the thickly padded chair and actually felt like he could relax for a bit. Greg, Frank and Shane sat behind him. They were all in a deep discussion about expanding their company's internet presence.

Daniel wondered how he could quietly move, but all the seats were taken. He was stuck listening to Greg pontificate.

The game was moving at a leisurely pace, well into the third inning and still no hits. Daniel had tried to ignore Greg's endless ramblings. He wondered why Gary had brought this eclectic group together.

"So Danny, tell me what's on your mind, besides the trial." Gary leaned in close. Daniel was startled for a moment, he had been zoned out.

"Well, I can't think of much else but the trial. I don't know what the media attention is going to do to the approval process."

"Don't you have a crack team of legal experts over there?" Gary asked.

"Of course, but sometimes you have to wonder what they are up to. They seem like a pretty secretive group. How do I know what I don't know? What if they aren't telling us everything? How do you decide where the fine line between need to know and needless to know is?"

"Only you can decide that," Gary chuckled. "You are always one who seems to shy away from knowing every little detail. That's actually a great quality, otherwise, you'll get bogged down by minutia when you are in the position to be the big overall view guy. You are suited to that."

"Some days I'm not sure, I get really hung up on the feeling that I'm not qualified to run this entire organization. I get the feeling that there are a lot of people talking behind my back and I'm walking around oblivious. When I do ask, it seems that people seem defensive or worried that I suspect they aren't doing their jobs. I'm just trying to keep a finger on what's going on."

Greg's hand came down on Daniel's shoulder. "I feel your pain," he interrupted.

Daniel turned to see Greg leaning toward him. "I feel that way too, like there are a lot of plates to keep spinning. Or I should say, I felt that way. Always worried that I was missing something. It really comes down to trusting the people working for you."

"That's easier said than done," Shane added. "We were burned badly by some mid-level managers who were doing their own thing, basically setting their own policies, but still appearing to be team players on the surface. It took us quite a while to clean house. What's your advice on that?"

"I think you missed a great opportunity to engage a lot of creativity and come out with a better strategy," Greg said. Daniel tried not to roll his eyes. Oh no, he thought, he's an expert at everything.

"How so?" Shane shot back. "They were undermining senior management; that surely doesn't fly anywhere."

"Hear me out," Greg said. "One of the best things you can do in upper management is to set the tone for collaboration across all platforms. Put unlikely groups together to work on projects or challenges."

"How can you do that successfully? A lot of people are afraid to speak up when there are big egos in the room. Our brainstorming sessions don't usually produce any ground breaking ideas, they seem to just build on someone's initial suggestion. Everyone turns into yes men."

"It does take a while to change the culture. Senior management needs to be the lead. It can be done," Greg replied.

Daniel thought for a moment. He didn't like this guy, but he did have a point. "Suppose we put these odd groups together. Then what?" he asked.

"Stress the point that management wants to explore a number of viewpoints and options before making any decisions. Ask the newest hire and the most tenured to describe the company and what it does—many times it gives you some very surprising answers. Whatever you do, don't shut someone down. You may not like what you are hearing, and while it's certainly not the venue to express grievances, you can keep the discussion to overall solution-seeking." Greg replied.

"Isn't that just brainstorming?"

"It could turn into that, but as I said, senior management needs to set the tone and lead the discussion. Many times brainstorming turns into one person offering a suggestion and others agreeing that it sounds good. It doesn't get you very far. Instead of people calling out suggestions, have them work in pairs and write several solutions down, then pull them out of a hat and discuss as a group. Another way is to play devil's advocate. However, the person who is asking the question really needs to want to know others' observations. Approach it as the respondents are doing you a favor giving you their perspective. Discuss both sides, not only what could go wrong, but what could go well."

Shane was shaking his head frantically. "That surely hasn't been my experience. Anytime I've ever asked that question, I've been shot down pretty quick."

"But now you are in a position to change your company's culture. There are three things you can do in your position that set the tone for the entire organization, it makes your company what I like to call Brainiant – one that values everyone's input, perspective and creativity." Greg replied.

"What are the three things?" Clint asked. By now, all attention had turned to the discussion. The game was a quiet din in the distance.

"Questioning without confronting, answering without feeling defensive, and exploring a number of viewpoints and options before making a decision."

There was a moment of silence.

"Yeah, like that's simple," Clint said. "We have a lot of very defensive people in our organization."

"Many companies do, it hamstrings them terrifically. Everyone is afraid of making a mistake or admitting they don't know the answer. Imagine if that were turned around to everyone working together. Actually having an employee say to you, 'I made a mistake, but here is what I've found that will prevent that from happening, or here is how we can improve the process so it doesn't happen again.' If you were presented with that scenario, how would you respond?" Greg offered.

The men all gazed off into the distance and thought about what had been said. A loud crack shot through the air and the crowd erupted.

"A triple!" Clint yelled. Everyone was on their feet. It was the first good hit of the game.

The men watched for a while, yet Daniel was intrigued. He still thought Greg was a bit of a know it all, but maybe he was the one being defensive.

"So how do you propose to question without confronting? How can you ask someone why they did what they did without it coming off as a confrontation?" Daniel was thinking of all the times Harold would demand to know why he did what he did. It always made Daniel feel defensive and afraid, like he was still a 12 year old kid, called on the carpet for doing something wrong.

"I'm sure we've all been guilty of this. Say you want to know why a shipment was late. You probably already know the answer, but you want to test the supervisor. So you ask, waiting to hear the answer you knew was coming. You know, 'Why was the Smith order out late?' First, you are setting the tone. 'Why' questions tend to set us all off. It's almost like our days in elementary school, when the teacher was asking you a question, she was testing you. That doesn't fly in business, not if you want your employees to be forthcoming and creative problem solvers." Greg continued.

"Perhaps, but sometimes the best question is why." Shane said.

"You can still ask why, but from the point of seeking solutions, not placing blame. For instance, I approach Frank, 'The Kraft paper production seems to be falling behind deadline. Last I saw, we were positioned to be ahead of the seasonal demand. Where are we missing something?' He now feels engaged as part of the solution, rather than the whipping boy." Greg playfully elbowed Frank.

Daniel could only dream that Harold would phrase a question like that. "OK, say you are the one being asked. How do you answer without feeling defensive?" he asked.

"It's difficult to do, I know, but you can frame it with what you've discovered and a suggestion on how to correct it or improve it."

"Surely everyone struggles with this. I mean, a company is its own living, breathing thing. How do you make this sort of change in everyone's mindset? Especially the old guard. It's difficult to spread this touchy-feely, kum-by-ya stuff." Daniel added.

"It takes some time, but it is possible." Greg turned his attention back to the game. "Pierce is up, he needs to get a hit."

By the seventh inning stretch, Daniel was beginning to feel more optimistic. The idea of putting new work groups together was enthralling.

Gary had been absorbed in the game, keeping stats in his program.

"Hey, you've been quiet," Daniel nudged him.

Gary gave him a wink, "I didn't want to interrupt your conversation."

"You dog, you knew just what you were doing putting us together. What's this guy do, coaching on the side? Was this a tryout?" Daniel asked.

"Maybe, but regardless, I knew he'd have some good advice. He really turned around the old school thinking at a couple other companies. *Big* companies."

The crowd noise swelled, the men bolted up to see Pierce slide into home behind two other runners, clinching the game.

As the crowd began to file out of the stadium, Daniel stayed and talked with the other men. Greg and Frank had slipped out, but the rest of them all agreed they had heard some new ideas.

"I would love to implement the new type of work groups," Shane said. "I just don't know if I can sell it." The others nodded.

"I think we just approach it as a new solution, what is there to lose?

Bonus Stuff: Powerful questions dig deeper into a subject and bring up interesting ideas and options. Avoid asking questions as if you are testing someone to see if they know the answer you have in your head. There is no new information, ideas or combinations when you are just testing them. Powerful questions are open ended so that the person answering is free to take the subject in a new direction.

Questions are the sign of intelligence and a thirst for knowledge. Questions are the sign of an open mind, the ability to admit to yourself you don't know all the answers, and in fact, you may not know the answer to the specific topic. At the very least, there may be more options you haven't considered. For all those reasons, ask the question and then listen to the answer without judgment.

5 BREAD & SOUP

MOLLY WENT to a small strip mall near the motel and stocked up on some better coffee, a nice baguette and a couple containers of soup from the deli. That would hold her for a couple days. The basics.

As she pulled out of the parking lot, she noticed an internet café and bookstore across the street. She shot across the street, just missing an oncoming truck that honked its disapproval.

The man at the cash register smiled and nodded as she walked in. Suddenly she felt more relaxed than she had in days. She loved little places like this, she had just been so swamped at work that she hadn't taken time to browse around in a bookstore in months.

She wandered past the romance novels, giggling to herself at the silly sounding titles. She preferred autobiographies and how-to books, but her real weakness was how to use your brain. She passed the reference shelf and saw a book on brain games. Then she noticed a familiar name—the author was the same one that wrote the article she had torn out of the dentist's magazine. She flipped through a few pages, it went into more detail about mind maps, decision making, and creativity. She quickly turned and headed toward the cashier. This will do, she thought.

After she reached her room, she made herself a small lunch of the bread and one container of soup. Before the microwave finished cooking, she had already skimmed several pages of her new book. She skipped to the section on how your brain fools you.

"How your brain tricks you:

Our brains can trick us into believing the wrong things at times. If you can't trust your own brain whose brain should you trust? The extent of each of the tricks it plays are dependent in part on your thinking style. The other part is that your brain has developed protective measures and efficiency techniques that can lead it astray.

It recognizes and sees what it expects to see. Expectations are so strong an influence that it is not unusual for a person to insist they saw something that wasn't there - or didn't see something that was there. For instance, a person sees a video, but missed an important part or didn't see it correctly. When they are told what really happened, they will often deny vehemently until the evidence is so strong that they have no choice. And they still may walk away grumbling that they believe a trick was played on them even though they have no idea how they could have made that mistake."

Wow, that's Harold to a T, Molly thought. It was always difficult to correct him if he had misunderstood a chart or report. Daniel would just give up, but then Harold would ask Molly to verify—leaving her in a difficult position.

"Our brain wants to jump to the first solution to a problem. Our years in school have taught us that there is one right solution, unfortunately. Once we think of a solution to a business problem we might feel that we are done. But in business and in life in general, problems may have many potential solutions and the first one you think of may not turn out to be the best one. In fact, the first solution tends to be the most common one and certainly not the most innovative you can come up with."

Molly took another sip of the soup. This entire book was so in line with what was happening at the office. Even with Harold removed as CEO, there was still a tremendous power struggle between him and Daniel.

"Your filters and perceptions color everything you see. From the time you were born

your brain had to learn to filter out unimportant details and focus on important ones. However, what is important may change over time. Your filters may lead you astray by missing something you thought at one time was unimportant but now should attract your attention. In addition, our brains believe that others must be seeing the world the same way. Not ideologies, since most of the time we admit to differences, but what we think we saw or heard. What came in through our senses? We think that has to be the same for all. But it's not."

Molly felt a tug in her gut. What had she missed that was unimportant but now had her attention? She thought back to the time of Fred Hirsh's accident. Everyone was stunned by his death, but she couldn't shake the feeling that something was fishy. Fred was a great innovator, always on the lookout for new ideas, new strategies and direction for the company. He wasn't afraid to suggest new things, and since he was production and development, it was expected. However, everything was tied up too neatly when he went away on his trip. Summaries on various projects were complete, emails were all handled, and his notes were all on the shared drive. It was if he knew he wasn't coming back.

It seemed that Brad was against filling the position too quickly, which was also odd, since he was head of Finance, but she had overhead him telling Daniel to take his time filling the position. He claimed it was out of respect to Fred.

She read on: *"Focus forces you to miss what's on the periphery. If something does attract your attention such as a cute dog, unusual situation, or something bright and sparkly, you lose track of whatever you were thinking about just prior to the distraction."*

Harold was all about focus. In the days when she first worked at Wilson-Shaw, Harold would manage by walking around and talking with everyone, encouraging them to stay focused and keep up the good work. Molly could focus when she needed to, but she enjoyed the chance to let her mind wander and think of new ideas. Others joked that she was ADD, but she knew she wasn't, just easily intrigued by the unexpected.

"Multitasking means nothing gets your complete focus. Even though business people brag about multitasking as if it is a good thing, it prevents you from keeping your focus on what is important long enough to get it completed. Our brains are so easily distracted."

Ok, maybe I'm guilty of that one, she thought. Yet there were often so many things happening at once, it was important to keep Daniel in line. She knew his escape was running, and when he came back to the office, he could be immersed in his work for several hours afterward.

"Statistics don't lie, but liars quote statistics, and they may be absolutely certain that they are not lying. You can listen to two different politicians or news broadcasters telling the same story and it sounds like there is a different conclusion. It is possible to interpret situations differently and our brains seek out the pieces that support its preferred conclusion. It's called confirmation bias and most of the time we don't realize we have it."

Wow, this was the board of directors, she thought. Every time there seemed to be disagreement between the board and Daniel and Harold, the statistics flew like arrows. There was a lot of animosity between them, it didn't make sense. They all wanted the company to be profitable, didn't they?

"Flight or fight reaction to a threat. It doesn't have to be a physical threat for our brain to react with either flight or fight. Your brain may lash out with its own interpretation of the situation. In others it may withdraw, shrug shoulders, and change the subject or walk away."

Yup, that's Daniel, she thought. Thank goodness for treadmills and cell phones, otherwise he would be missing in action more than she could cover.

"Prejudice about a topic. Once the brain makes up something it sounds like it must be true. After all, it is still sitting there in the brain to be retrieved as needed. Judgment may be based on a small amount of information or even misinformation, but stated often enough, even if only thought, it gets more real."

That was one of Fred's favorite sayings, Molly remembered. "If you say it with enough conviction, it must be true," he'd joke. While he joked about it, it was often what happened. An idea would ripple throughout the VPs and they would all buy in, even if there were no hard data. Fred would get such a kick out of it.

"It treats risk as something to avoid, or for some people, something that adds excitement to life, as in playing blackjack or driving too fast.

It makes assumptions all the time and then we may not remember that we didn't really have all the facts. If we learn to recognize when we make assumptions because we don't have access to all the facts at that moment, we can admit and be ready to reconsider when new information becomes available."

Molly took another sip, the soup was cold. The churning in her stomach wasn't due to hunger, it was the realization that she was smack in the middle of a huge swirl of conflict between Daniel, his dad and the rest of the company. By disappearing, it was going to be even worse. She still didn't know if or how she could go back.

Bonus Stuff: Have you ever driven to work only to find yourself pulling into your parking spot and realizing you have no memory of the drive? What happened?

Your brain was more or less on autopilot, focusing on something else while you were driving. Luckily for most people, if there is something that demands full concentration, your brain will jump to attention. If you need to be paying full attention to a situation, conversation, or the road, you need to put your brain into attentive mode and not let it wander.

Our brain also fools us by using selective memory. You may have discovered that you and associates at work remember a situation differently. It may be about who was in attendance, how long the meeting continued, or whether or not a particular decision was made. Taking notes can help, but we also need to recognize when we may not all be interpreting a discussion the same way. Too often we see or hear what we were expecting rather than what actually happened.

A decision discussed and completed must be stated as such, may require paraphrasing, and getting participants to acknowledge and agree.

6 BUS STOP

HEADING INTO WORK the next morning, Daniel found himself behind the school bus again. He didn't mind, he was still thinking about his conversation with Greg at the game. Even though Wilson-Shaw was in the business of creating a new drug, he wasn't sure the company culture was one that encouraged a lot of creativity. Fred had been a leader in that area, integrating unusual work groups, keeping a journal of all kinds of ideas and taking those hikes which he said cleared out the cobwebs and let the 'new stuff' in.

While there were stringent safety guidelines, it seemed that sometimes the board was overly hung up on staying within the parameters too early in the game.

He thought about it while he watched the bus come to another stop. Moms and their kids were waiting for the door to open. One boy was bouncing around, hopping from one foot to another, while a little girl watched him warily, tightly holding her mother's hand. Two of the bigger kids stood away from their mothers. He remembered how they had huddled together earlier in the winter to stay warm while waiting for the bus. An odd group, he thought. One very active, two who seem too old, and a small girl too afraid to break away from her mom. He wondered how that would translate to a work group. Would the shy girl feel comfortable enough to make suggestions? How do you draw someone out like that? Or do you not hire them in the first place? And what about that kid bouncing around? At what point is that shushed out of him so he becomes quiet and afraid to think up new games or activities? Are we doing that at Wilson-Shaw?

Brad's face was the first thing Daniel saw as the elevator doors opened. "Hey," Daniel blurted.

"Hey yourself, we've got to talk," Brad replied as he walked along side Daniel to his office. "The values are all over the place, the morning figures had us up too high, we can't sustain that type of growth. We need the price to drop so more shares can be sold."

"Brad, you may be the numbers guy, but I don't understand how that will help us. Do we really need more shareholders at the moment? Can't the value just go up and those that already hold our stock can make some money?"

"It sounds logical, but we have unsold shares that need to be purchased. Lowering the stock would solve that problem," Brad's voice was nearly breathless. Daniel noticed that twinge in his gut and for once, it stopped him in his tracks.

"What's really going on?" Daniel shot back. He winced, so much for asking without confronting.

"We are just very vulnerable as a company at the moment," Brad answered. There was a buzzing sound and Brad took the phone out of his pocket. "Gotta go."

Brad spun around and scurried back down the hall. Daniel stood there for a moment. He didn't know Brad all that well and didn't really understand him, and the conversation surely didn't make sense. He shook his head and continued to his office. Brooke was at Molly's desk again.

"I'm surprised to see you," he said.

"I know you are. I'm not sure what is happening with Molly. HR called me just a few minutes ago to let me know you needed coverage again today," Brooke smiled. Daniel bristled at the idea, then realized that a new perspective could be as close as his own assistant.

"Great, we have a lot of work to do today," he said.

"Then let's get started!" she followed him into his office, tablet in hand.

"I have several things I need you to research for me. First, the actress—any leads?" Before she could answer, Daniel continued. "Then there is a company called, Green Planet, I think that's it. They are a recycling company here in town. Also, a man named Greg." Daniel realized that he didn't remember his last name. He never missed things like that.

"Ah, I don't remember Greg's last name, but if you call Gary Brownlee and ask him, he can get you the info. I want to know his company name. Just don't tell Gary that you are researching him."

Daniel sat down at his computer and began to scan his emails. There was a request to connect on LinkedIn from none other than Frank—Greg's cohort at the baseball game yesterday. Daniel studied Frank's profile. It didn't say anything about a company, just consulting to Fortune 100 companies. He scanned through his connections, but Greg's name and photo didn't show. Daniel thought that was odd. He clicked accept and moved on to another email that caught his eye.

Trident Think Tank Openings

He clicked and began to read. *Do you engage your employees when seeking creative solutions to roadblocks, or do you go it alone? When was your last breakthrough? Trident Think Tank, recognized as the business world's most innovative portal matches corporate authorities and executives with premier level leaders who generously donate their expertise and mentoring to the next generation. Trident mentors serve with the idea that sharing ideas and strategies benefit the entire world when business leaders embrace creativity and productivity in non-traditional ways. As CEO of Wilson-Shaw, you have been selected to complete the application process. We welcome your participation and hope that you will join us in this exclusive, dynamic and collaborative community.*

Daniel leaned back in his chair. He read it again. He knew of Trident, but had no idea they knew of him. You couldn't apply without an invitation, and here it was. He stared out the window, there were several people at the bus stop below. He thought about the school children he saw earlier. A small group, but each one was avoiding the other. It was the same with the people below. Everyone kept their distance. One woman was talking on her phone, another was sitting on the bench, arms tightly folded. Two men stood nearby, but even they kept their distance from one another.

There could be the makings of a million dollar deal down there, but no one will talk to anyone, he thought. He reflected on the conversation at the ball game. He was all enthused about changing the corporate culture at Wilson-Shaw. He had tried before, but perhaps he was too abrupt. Starting on a smaller scale, with the lab groups and lower level employees might be the way to go.

"Brooke," he called.

"Yes sir, I've got the name of the actress' agent." She replied.

"Great, I'll take that, but I have another project for you to set up as well. I need a meeting with the department VPs. Tell them it is 20 minutes only, outside in the garden this afternoon. No notebooks, electronic devices, nothing."

Brooke tried to hide her bewilderment, but nodded her head. "I'm on it."

That will shake things up. The pile of papers on his desk began to rattle and buzz. Checking his pockets, he realized his phone was buried under there. He fished through the papers and answered.

"Hi Dad."

Bonus Stuff: How unique does an idea have to be to be considered creative? Is an idea totally new to you but not new to the world an example of creativity? Are small changes good enough to be called creativity?

The patent office deals with this question in a legal capacity but for our purposes here we are looking at the subject in a more general way because most of what we develop and think up are ideas that can be applied in ways that don't get patented. Though sometimes they do apply to copyright.

A song that has a new refrain or new lyrics yet uses the same words in new combinations, is that creativity? Solving a problem in a new way but with the same ultimate answer, is that creativity?

Enough questions. I think you get the idea. It is a slippery slope.

In general, seeing anything in a new way, new combinations, previously unknown to you, can be considered creative. If it is known to the world, your creation may never make any money nor even be credited to you but it is still a sign of your creativity.

Bull Ship by Will Bullas

7 BLAME SHAME

BROOKE FOUND links and phone numbers to Melanie Meyer's agent and social media page. Daniel wasn't one for tweeting and Facebooking, but he was skeptical that Melanie was actually posting personal things. There were photos of fancy salads, comments about auditioning for roles, and her workouts. Oddly enough, there was no mention of RQ246 on any of the websites.

He dialed the agent's number, it went immediately to voicemail. Before he could leave a message, his phone beeped with an incoming call.

By noon, Daniel felt so skittish he couldn't sit still. Brooke had scheduled the VP meeting for 3:30 so he knew he could get a run in and think his plan through. He logged off his computer. As he walked through the office he saw Brad outside his office door on his cell. Brad gave a startled nod, then turned his back and kept the phone to his ear. Daniel shook his head and pushed the stairwell door open. He was dashing down the stairs, rounded the corner and saw one of the lab assistants standing there talking on her phone. As she saw Daniel, her eyes grew wide. He smiled and continued on. He didn't know who she was, only that her blue lab coat identified her as assistant to a senior researcher. He wondered what the policy on personal calls in the workspace was. He realized he didn't know. Maybe that was what Brad was doing talking in the hallway.

He walked through the lobby and nodded at the security guard. "Good afternoon Mr. Shaw."

Even though Wilson-Shaw had gym facilities on site, Daniel preferred the club a few blocks away. He liked seeing others who weren't part of the company. He especially liked the pick-up basketball games with the group of guys that had no idea who he was or the size of the company he ran. It was a bit of anonymity that he enjoyed.

Once upstairs on the treadmills, Daniel changed the channel on one of the TVs. It was the noon business report featuring a story on two college students with a startup company based on a new app. The stock prices scrawled across the bottom of the screen. For some reason, everything was down today. He tried to read the fine print, but couldn't make it out. Instead, he looked out the window and cranked up the intensity. He wondered what the look on his direct report's faces would be when they gathered in the courtyard later that afternoon. He wanted to shake things up a bit and it seemed like a good place to start. Get out of the stuffy conference room and out in the open. Daniel wasn't a micro-manager, he believed his VPs were skilled and competent and he let them run their departments with little interference. On the other hand, his Dad barely let Daniel breathe without reporting directly back to him. It was a frustrating position, Harold still behaved as if he ran the company. Daniel originally thought the consulting position would be a good idea and something to help keep Harold occupied after Mom's death. Daniel couldn't bear the thought of his Dad being so distraught and aimless. Now it seemed to have backfired. Harold ordered Daniel around, questioned every decision, and doubted his ability. Daniel had enough doubts on his own, a little support from his dad would go a long way. Perhaps that was a conversation they could have one day, when Daniel got the nerve.

As he continued to pound out the miles, Daniel contemplated the invitation from Trident. To turn down the opportunity would be professional suicide. They were coveted invitations. However, it would take a lot of time if he were selected. He was getting ahead of himself, the application and interview process were time consuming enough. Still, he realized he couldn't let that chance slip away. He'd get started on the application right after the meeting.

By 3:30, the sun had warmed the pavers in the courtyard and the buds on the trees were green and ready to burst open. The air had a delicious promise of spring. As the company VPs filtered into the courtyard, they all had the same puzzled expression.

"How many of you have even been in this courtyard before?" Daniel asked with his hand up. No hands raised. "Yes, the same for me. I realized that we have this beautiful area that only the landscape company visits. I'll be the first to admit, I'd much rather be out here than behind my desk. Especially on a day like today. It's been a long, cold winter. Today is one of those days you can almost taste, spring is on the way."

One of the men chuckled under his breath and turned away. Daniel began to wonder if this was a good idea after all.

"I realize this is unorthodox, but we have fallen into a rut. We sit around that big, glossy conference table and everyone acts as if they are engaged in the discussion, when in fact, they are checking email or scrolling through the sports news on their devices. I'm not blaming anyone, we've all done it. It's time that stopped. We are all part of one company, and far too often we behave as separate entities. In order to keep the heat off our department, we'll deflect and play the blame/shame game by throwing another department under the bus." Heads cautiously began to nod in agreement.

"Something struck me today while I was running at the gym. On the news was a story about two 19 year-old kids that have a multi-million dollar start up just from an idea for an app. Imagine, two guys, kicking an idea around in their dorm room and then going for it. Creativity and technology are taking off like never before. Sometimes I think it gets bogged down in org charts and corporate red tape when we work at this level."

Daniel could feel the warmth of the sun on the back of his neck. Two of the men slipped off their jackets and unbuttoned their shirt sleeves. People were beginning to relax, yet more interested and engaged than he'd ever seen them.

"So how does that equate to us standing here, outside the boardroom?" One asked.

"I wanted to make a point, and set a precedent. We are a company that works to improve people's health. We research and test and eventually manufacture a product that can heal or even save a life. It's an incredible mission when you think about it. Yet, I think we have become so engrossed in the bottom line that we stifle the ideas and creativity to consider other ways to help people be healthy. This courtyard is one example. It's been proven that blood pressure and stress levels go down when you get outdoors. Granted, this is only a small courtyard, but it's here. There are birds, trees, flowers and in a few more weeks, I'm sure the fountain will be running again. Listen."

The group looked around. "I don't hear anything," one of the women said.

"Exactly," Daniel answered. "There is no street noise. We are in the middle of the city, yet this courtyard is quiet. Where else can you get that? We don't have any pinging from email, no phones buzzing. We have quiet. Now, I promised this would only take 20 minutes out of your day. I want to present a challenge to all of you and then I'd like you to take the remainder of the time to just soak up the sunshine, get some fresh air and consider what I'm about to say."

Skeptical faces now looked eager.

"We have some very forward thinking work groups. RQ246 is a direct result of great collaboration. I'd like to continue to build on that momentum, but change things up a bit. Have your most recent hire and the most senior employee write a brief description about what they think they do and how it contributes to the company. Read those descriptions at the meeting, but don't identify who wrote it. Compare that to what the others in the work group think they do. Emphasize that there is no right or wrong answer, they are just differing perspectives on what your department does. I'd like to hear what the results are at our next gathering. Thank you for your time, and enjoy it out here."

Daniel walked away quickly so no one had time to question the task. He wanted to see how they handled it.

He was feeling pretty good about the idea as he walked into his office. Brad and Brooke were both standing there, mouths agape, watching the TV. Daniel studied the screen; it was Melanie Meyers. Dark glasses, scraggly hair and a hat pulled low, "It's devastating, I'm losing my hair, my skin is on fire. I feel terrible. I blame it all on Wilson-Shaw. Shame on you, you call yourselves a drug company?"

Bonus Stuff: We often undervalue and underestimate the work others do, even in our own organization. Years ago a coworker constantly made sarcastic remarks about my job. It was painful. But I must admit I didn't think he did much to earn his salary either. It always seemed to me that all he did was take data reports and put together summaries of what he was provided. It never seemed to me that he did anything productive. And that was what he accused me of as well. My personality was to keep those thoughts to myself while his was to be vocal about it.

Too often we feel no one works as hard as we do. How do we get past this? Step back and ask sincere questions about what they do so you can support each other better. Step into each other's shoes virtually (or if possible actually exchange jobs temporarily) and get a feel for what needs to get done each day, what the stressors are, and how important cooperation and networking are for the success of the job. When we do, relationships will be easier and more productive.

Call of the Wild by Will Bullas

8 BOLD SOLUTION

Low clouds hung in the distance. The sun was peeking through occasionally, causing the light in Molly's room to make it difficult to read. The bedside lamp was burned out and she hadn't bothered to tell the front desk. She wanted to get outside and walk a bit. She needed to figure out if and when she was going back to work. She was sure that it would be much too difficult to explain things to Daniel. She considered making up some exotic illness or rough bout of flu, but everyone knew she never missed work, even when she was under the weather.

Her cell phone was blinking with additional texts and missed calls. Harold had called two more times. His messages were now short and sweet. "Kiddo, hope all is ok, please check in."

He was a protective father figure to her even if he was difficult to deal with. Other assistants would keep their distance, but over the years, she had been able to figure him out. She would just let him spew for a while, then wait for him to calm down before answering him. It was a strategy that had served her very well.

She had avoided all internet, news or TV since she disappeared. She walked to the front desk to ask for a new light bulb. The 24 hour news station was playing in the corner of the kitchenette. A familiar face was on the screen, yet it was pale, splotchy and covered by dark glasses. Molly stared for a moment, then the caption below the photo froze her in her tracks: it was Melanie Meyers.

Molly wheeled around and headed back to her room. Her heart raced. It's happening, it's really happening. Wilson-Shaw is going to crash and burn, she thought.

She turned the deadbolt on her hotel room door. She had felt safe here and convinced that no one would know where she was. She had been diligent to not respond to calls or texts. Now she felt nervous and flighty. She didn't like that about herself, she was usually able to put on a brave front at work, the ever confident and resourceful Molly.

Pacing around the room, she decided to make some notes. She flipped through the book back to a section on decision making that she had read earlier. Perhaps one of the exercises would help her sort things out.

"Simple vs Complex Decisions. Simple decisions require the same steps as complex ones, except there are fewer, better known options, so they are often made in split seconds without a lot of deliberation."

Molly swallowed hard. Maybe she hadn't given this a lot of thought. She needed to revise her plan, the question was how.

"Problem solving -*In school you more than likely solved problems in math and other subjects where the purpose was to find the one answer in the back of the book or that your teacher had in mind - usually only one right answer. Now move yourself forward to today. Your work, your life, the world has umpteen problems to solve. If you treat them all like they taught you in school you will quit when you come up with an answer because* *you would think there is only one answer. In real life there are many answers to most problems, some better, some more creative, some easier, some more competitive, some will make more money, some will do a better job of CYA, or whatever. Problem solving is very different now. Your job is to be creative, come up with multiple options and then understand the constraints or priorities to help you make good choices.*

You need tools and methods to renew your thought processes and be able to become a good option-thinker. It's a different process than looking for one right answer at the back of the book.

This may require brainstorming, either on your own or with a group of people who would think about the same problem in very different ways. Recognizing thinking style differences and attracting a team of 'think different' people will make the brainstorming extra productive and diverse."

Great idea, Molly thought, but I'm hanging out here by myself.

"Breaking a problem into its smaller components often makes it easier to solve piece by piece and may even yield a breakthrough you didn't see when you were trying to solve it as one big whole."

The author, with an extensive background in teaching mathematics, went on to describe how companies and individuals can solve problems. It was clear she felt strongly that learning to get the right answer wasn't as important as developing the problem solving skills and confidence that went along with it. Molly wished she had had a teacher like that, she had struggled with math all through school and would be especially frustrated when she would lose points on a portion of the answer.

"From learning and teaching mathematics, the ultimate and straight-forward problem solving exercise, it became painfully apparent that the reason so many young people have trouble with math is because they learn an answer to a problem but they don't always learn problem solving methods they can use over and over. Think about math text books. They go through a technique with an example or two and then most of the problems looked exactly the same. Just plug in the answers. The ultimate goal was to avoid a big red X— wrong answer.

When helping my own children with their math homework they were often frustrated because I wouldn't just give them answers. Instead I'd ask questions about how and why one would do certain steps and 'what if' questions to look at variations. In teaching math classes, I would ask, how did you get that answer?"

Molly put down the book. She knew she had gotten her answer. It was a shaky plan, hastily concocted and one she was beginning to regret more every day. Now her brain was roiling, searching for either an answer, or the nerve to back out of the plan.

"Striving for strength, flexibility, and resilience are attributes for your brain as much as the muscles in your arms and legs. Improve your brain by keeping it well rested, well oxygenated by breathing deeply, and doing something aerobic every day. Stress and being tired is bad for the brain, calming methods such as yoga and deep breathing are effective.

Lack of use is also detrimental. Keep it exercised by learning something new every day.

If you are working your brain hard because you have a big project to complete or something that requires focus for a long time, take a short break every hour. Just like you should get up from a chair at least once an hour for a five minute muscle break, switch to a different activity, listen to music, look at some calming pictures or even better, take a short walk outside, which will exercise and relax body and mind at the same time."

Molly leaned back and looked back over the ocean. She let her mind wander as she watched the surf ebb and flow. She closed her eyes and listened to the sounds. She hadn't been to the beach in several years, she wanted to savor the sounds and smells.

Maybe she should just call in to work and talk to Daniel. Tell him that she was exhausted and needed another day or so to get it together. Maybe she should just jump in the car and drive and see where she ended up. Maybe not, she sighed. For now, she would keep reading, perhaps her next move may come to her.

She opened the book to the section on mind maps.

"How does color equate to business and your brain? We all react to colors and often we will have similar reactions, such as feeling calm when seeing the blue of the sky or in a room painted a soothing shade. We associate red with warning us of peril and stop signs. Green means go to most of us because of traffic lights. What does purple bring to mind for you? How about pink? Aqua? The right colors can improve mood and the use of multiple colors in a mind map can energize the process. Color also improves recall as you may be able to prove for yourself as you work to remember past situations, you will find that when you can picture the colors it helps the whole memory flood back."

Molly had always been intrigued by the idea of mind maps. She often worked on them with Daniel, especially since he liked to work his way through a problem by actually moving through it.

"Most people are visual in their dealing with the world around them. We can remember what a room looked like better than we can remember people's names. Colors in the picture help us remember even better."

She looked around the dingy hotel room. This color is anything but inspiring, she thought. She flipped through her journal to a clean page. She drew a circle in the middle and labeled it "Choices". She drew three smaller circles around it and labeled them "Go Back", "Disappear" and "Stick with Plan." She chewed the end of the pen while she considered the pros and cons of each choice. As each thought popped into her mind, she wrote them around the corresponding circle. She remembered reading the suggestion to use various colors in a mind map, but all she had with her was a blue ballpoint. It would have to do, she just needed to think things through, maybe get her nerve back.

No, she thought. I can work this out. I've gone this far, I'll stay with the plan.

Bonus Stuff: Learning how to pare down a subject to keywords is a skill worth cultivating. It helps us focus on what's most important. Mind Mapping, also known as idea mapping, and brain blooms, is a visual way to think things through. Mind maps:

- Help us use keywords, symbols, or pictures the way our brain needs
- Gets rid of extraneous information that may cloud the issue and your mind
- Make your notes clear, concise, and complete
- Help you communicate more effectively with others
- Make it easier to follow your thoughts and decision process
- Help you naturally create an executive summary
- Are appreciated by busy business people everywhere

In addition, mind mapping improves your memory for the subject.

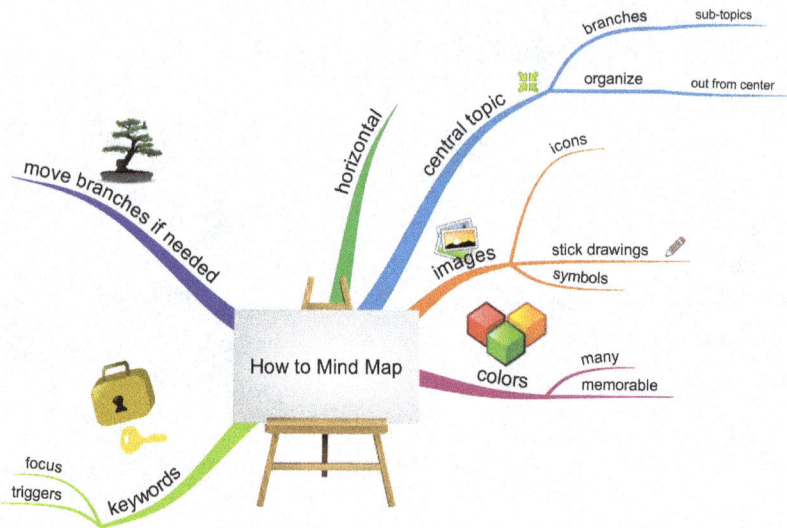

Effective mind maps:

1. Create relationships on paper in the manner your brain stores and recalls.

2. Builds deeper understanding as the mind map develops on the paper

3. Easier to explain to others

4. Organizes your thoughts

5. Gets more done in less time

6. Efficient note taking

7. Efficient note making

8. Natural brainstorming

9. Creativity blossoms

10. Is more fun

9 BAND-AID SUCCESS

Daniel got up before CeeCee and headed to the gym. He nabbed a treadmill upstairs before the rush and was well into his run as the gym grew crowded. He watched the people below at the bus stop and thought about his goals for the day. His voicemail was full of calls from everyone from the *Wall Street Journal* and *Pharmacy News* to board members and Harold. It would be full-on damage control today.

Hopefully Molly would show up, she had never missed two consecutive days of work. He needed to find out what was going on with her. He put other people to work on the press releases for RQ246, he had no other choice. He needed to have Brad and the legal department in the same room to discuss the financial stability of the company now that the publicity was causing values to swing so wildly. He also didn't want to procrastinate on the Trident application. It was going to be a full day, but first the run to clear his head and feel energized.

He went to the locker room, showered, dressed, and set out for the office feeling confident and energetic.

When he arrived at the office, Brooke was at Molly's desk.

"Again?" he asked.

"I'm afraid so. She isn't answering calls, texts or emails. Do you think something happened to her? Should we do something?" Brooke asked.

"I'm not sure what we can do," Daniel answered.

"We could ping her cell phone."

Daniel wheeled around to see Brad in his office. "Do what?"

"Ping her cell. One of the IT guys could do it. They get a reading on the nearest cell tower that her phone is connected to," Brad answered.

"But she's not answering calls or texts," Brooke said nervously. "I've tried again this morning, but there's no response."

"It's your call Dan, but it's probably nothing," Brad turned to leave.

"Wait a minute, did you need something?" Daniel asked.

"Just leaving the mockup of the annual report on your desk. I've got a department meeting now, we can talk about this after you've had a chance to look it over. Besides, I think you've got your hands full with this latest Hollywood Minute," he shot back over his shoulder.

Daniel stood still for a moment and closed his eyes. Something seemed odd. Every time he talked with Brad he sensed it, almost like an invisible wall.

"What do you want to do about Molly?" Brooke asked again, breaking his concentration.

"I don't know, let me take care of a couple things first and then we'll figure out what to do." Daniel practically closed his office door in Brooke's face.

He leaned back in his chair and closed his eyes again. He ran the series of events through his mind. Molly's absence, the Hollywood leak, and the unusual vibe he got every time Brad was around. He shot forward and grabbed his pen, and began to jot notes on his blotter.

Molly—find her

Hollywood—what does this mean?

Brad—break down the weird wall.

He looked back over the list. Three very distinct issues, what was the commonality? Other than not knowing what was going on, they didn't seem connected. Molly never missed work. She would work from home if she was ever too sick to come in, but he couldn't remember the last time that happened.

The Hollywood leak—it was too fishy that they couldn't locate the publicist. He had the legal team investigating too, but no one seemed to know what was going on. If the bad news had the same influence on market shares, they could be crushed or taken over by the week's end. It was times like these that he could use a mentor. He wished that he could talk to Harold without it turning into a power struggle between father and son.

He scrolled through the numbers on his phone. Gary would be a good sounding board, he thought. He tapped the screen and waited for the call to connect. It went straight to voicemail.

Daniel let out a big sigh, "Gary, give me a call. Things are heating up here and I need an ear, or shoulder, or both."

As he dropped his phone on the desk, he noticed the other list he made when he woke up two nights ago.

The leak

Annual Report

Drug trial

College fund for Katie

Oil change

Molly's mysterious absence

Left knee is sore again

He drew a line through the last one. The soreness was gone. The leak remained at the top of the list.

One thing at a time, he said to himself. He walked past Brooke, "I'm heading over to legal."

The corridor to the legal department featured a wide angle view of the courtyard below. The freshly watered bushes were sparkling in the early morning sun. Daniel noticed that it was greener than it was during the meeting a couple days ago. He wondered if anyone had taken him up on the idea of having stand-up meetings in the courtyard.

Just as he reached the double doors to the legal department, he bumped into Brad who was on his way out. Brad's left eyebrow arced in surprise.

"I thought you had a finance department meeting," Daniel growled.

"Dude, I just needed to run down here to ask a question. I am trying to do damage control before this gets out of hand. Shareholders are dumping stock, we have pensions tied to the value. I need to know our position before it hits the fan."

"Then come back in here with me," Daniel ordered. "We need to all be on the same page."

Daniel and Brad entered the office of head counsel. Vaughn, the head of legal, was a small man, but built like a Mac truck. He was known for being a bulldog in court, but when the opportunity came along to work at Wilson-Shaw, he gave up courtroom drama for corporate law.

"Vaughn, what do we know about the impact of the Hollywood comments? Not only are we in a financially precarious situation, are we in jeopardy of losing the approval?" Daniel asked.

The high-backed leather chair dwarfed Vaughn, who cleared his throat and began to speak. "Once we locate Ms. Meyers, we will issue a cease and desist letter for her not to make any other remarks. It is too soon to determine the full extent of the financial shift based on her comments, however, we could sue for damages if it is found to be a result of her reckless commentaries. I recommend that we release a statement that Ms. Meyers is not affiliated to us in any way, and the very essence of a drug trial is that it is a blind study, therefore we cannot confirm that she is affiliated in any way with RQ246. That should right the ship, so to speak."

Brad nodded in agreement and turned to leave.

"Hold up," Daniel held up his hand. "That doesn't address the issue of the drop in value. Just issuing a statement won't help nervous stockholders." He looked Brad straight in the eye. "I don't hear you adding anything to the discussion. What is your position?"

Brad's eyes darted nervously around the room. "I've maintained from the start that the remarks are without merit and we are not in contact or in partnership with this girl, um, actress. You've been copied on the emails to the board and shareholders."

Both men noticed Vaughn studying them closely. Daniel lowered his hand and turned so Brad could leave.

After a moment, Daniel turned back to Vaughn. "Does something seem off with him?"

Vaughn turned his head slightly. "How so? He has been in contact with me ever since this Hollywood nonsense began. Everything has been right in line."

"It must be me," Daniel replied. "We'll keep digging to find Ms. Meyers and get this nipped in the bud so we can get our drug to market and make some real money." His phone began to buzz. He nodded to Vaughn and left the office.

"Mr. Shaw, I understand that you need an ear and a shoulder, would a beer do?" asked a familiar voice on the phone.

Daniel smiled. "Well, yes that would. I need some time to bounce a few things off of you. If you have time this week that would be just the ticket."

"I've always got time for you, my friend. I'm down at the coast, finishing up a golf outing today with some prospects," Gary said. "I will be back in town the day after tomorrow. Can it wait until then or would you like to take a long drive and meet me somewhere half way later today?"

"I'd rather not wait. I can meet you for a late dinner, then I'll just get a room somewhere and drive back early tomorrow. I could use a bit of a drive to think things through without interruptions." Daniel said.

"Great, let me know when you're on the road and I'll send you the address of a little place along the beach with great steaks. I think you could use a night out to bounce business ideas and challenges around," Gary chuckled.

Daniel hurried back to his office. He had a lot to get off his desk before he took off. He set a timer and told Brooke to hold all calls and visitors. The idea of time to sit and talk with Gary gave him motivation to get things done. He respected Gary's experience and opinion, the fact that there was a nice steak and a cold brew included made it all the more enticing.

He had just finished proofing the annual report when his cell phone rang. It was Harold.

"Hello Dad."

"Danny, what are you doing about that announcement yesterday? Where are we on stock values? I've had two board members call me wanting answers. I told them you were in charge, but your secretary is holding your calls."

"Legal is issuing a statement that we are not affiliated with the actress and that the proper trial protocol is a blind study, therefore she is only speculating what drug she received."

"You're going to have to appear on camera and make the statement," his dad urged. "It's the only way to head this off."

"Dad, I disagree. We release the statement through the legal department and let public affairs do the proper spin campaign. We respond as an institution, not an individual."

The line went silent. Daniel thought the call had dropped.

"Well son, I think that's a good decision. I'll let you handle this. I suppose I have been riding you too hard lately. I know you are on top of things. I know none of us saw this coming. The legal department is top-notch. I'll let you get back to it, talk to you later," Harold said.

Daniel looked at the phone. Did he really hear that right? Harold thinks he made a good decision? Amazing, he thought.

He checked the clock, he had time to begin the Trident application before meeting Gary. Scanning through the questions, a few caught his eye:

When faced with a decision, how do you proceed? Sometimes by the seat of my pants, he thought.

Another, How confident are you in your role as leader? "Depends on the day," he murmured.

He skipped to the essay portion. Describe your current leadership style and how you would like to change or improve it.

I strive to maximize the effectiveness of my team, however, I am not always confident that I encourage them to succeed. Since many of my colleagues are my peers, I sometimes over-think my ability to be in charge. I know they are extremely skilled in their respective areas. However, I do feel that I am able to motivate others to contribute and engage authentically and I reinforce the value of our collective energy as a team.

He read back over the statement. He'd think about it more while he drove. By the time he had cleared his desk and gone through his emails, it was later than he thought. He needed to get started on the road if he wanted to meet up with Gary tonight. He buzzed Molly's desk. "Yes?" Brooke answered.

Suddenly he remembered, he hadn't done anything about Molly. Brooke appeared at the office door.

"I'm sorry, we didn't make any progress on contacting Molly today, did we?" he asked.

"I never heard anything back, I was hoping that you did," Brooke answered.

"I need to head out for a dinner meeting, I'll try to call her from the road," Daniel said.

"Sir, I'm really concerned. It's just not like her to disappear like this. I don't mean to sound alarmist, but when young single women disappear, it's usually not under good circumstances. I don't think she has anyone around that keeps an eye on her. Your dad has called me several times to see if we heard anything."

"I'll make some calls while I'm on the road. Brad mentioned something about pinging her cell phone. Call the IT guys and find out what that entails, then give me a call."

Daniel grabbed his go bag from his office closet. Time to hit the road.

He settled into the buttery leather seat and started the engine, he heard a rattle—his phone had slipped into the console atop the coins in the tray.

"Hey buddy," Gary's voice boomed at the other end.

"I'm just pulling out of the garage, where am I headed?" Daniel asked.

"There's a great little place near St. Mornay on Route 234. It should be a little over an hour drive for you." Gary answered.

"I'll make it less than an hour," Daniel teased. "I haven't had this baby full out on the highway in a long time."

"I'd watch if I were you, there were all kinds of cop cars all over the place on my way down Saturday. But hey, it's your decision."

"I'll keep an eye out, and we'll be knocking back a cold one before you know it."

Bonus Stuff: There are a number of organizations that bring together people in similar careers or jobs that function as a think tank or a safe space to discuss the tough parts of one's job. A C level job makes it hard to admit weaknesses and doubts even though a person wouldn't be human without them.

Some organizations require an invitation or a recommendation.

Some are very specific as to age, background, size of company, or other requirements that make them very exclusive. One of which is cost, but worth every penny if you can afford them and fit the profile.

There are also organizations that are not so difficult to join nor expensive, yet also have open opportunities to engage business discussions that can be mutually beneficial. The National Association of Women Business Owners (NAWBO), National Speakers Association (NSA) and many other specialty organizations provide large conferences and small group discussions. There are Chambers of Commerce in nearly every city where you can meet with other business people and you don't have to be the CEO or President. You can form an advisory group, kitchen cabinet, meet-up or just a regular coffee group. There are many smaller informal groups that come together on a regular basis to brainstorm and bounce ideas off each other, or share worries, visions, and breakthroughs. Your search can begin as close as your local library, community college or Chamber of Commerce.

Parable by Will Bullas

10 BEER & STEAK

The chair squeaked in protest under Molly's endless fidgeting. With a heavy sigh, she parted the ratty curtains with the tip of her pen and tried to focus on the scene. The surf tumbled and sprayed in the bright sunshine. She was tired of reading and needed to get out and move.

She pulled on her hooded sweatshirt and made a quick inspection in the mirror. Her hair could use some curl, but after walking on the beach it wouldn't matter anyway. Shoving her room key and her journal in her pocket, she caught the red blinking light of her cell phone out of the corner of her eye. She turned it over on the bed so the light wouldn't show, then went out the door.

She wanted to slip past the front desk unnoticed, the easily flustered clerk kept trying to make conversation when he saw her and Molly didn't want to talk. As she neared the front desk, she was relieved to see a family with two little boys checking into the motel. The boys were spinning around flying imaginary airplanes. Molly smiled, they reminded her of little boys she used to babysit in high school. She nodded to the desk clerk and went out the front door.

The crisp air on her face suddenly cleared the cobwebs. Molly realized she had been closed up in her room for too long. She trudged up over the dune and walked toward the water. Slipping out of her shoes, she rolled up her pant legs. The tide was starting to come in and the surf was cold. She resisted the urge to back away from the water, she wanted to feel the coolness come over her feet and tingle up her legs.

She stared out into the ocean and took a deep breath. The only sounds were the gulls and the pounding surf. I could stay here forever, she thought. I may have to if things don't work out right.

Her moment was interrupted by the squeals and shrieks of the two little boys from the lobby. They were running straight for the water and splashed her as they sped by. She laughed at their carefree spirit. The mother was walking up behind them.

"Wow, all that energy," Molly said to her.

"Yes, it's boundless," the mother laughed.

Molly turned to go back toward the hotel. Her stomach was growling, but she was out of the bread and soup she bought at the market. She remembered a small bar and grill near the bookstore, it was close enough to walk to. It would be nice to have a drink too, she thought.

As she entered the restaurant, a young server smiled and said hello. Molly nodded then turned toward the bar. The dark knotty pine made it feel warm and cozy, which was a nice change from the chill she got at the beach. She ordered a gin and tonic from the bar, took her drink and slid into a booth at the far end of the room.

She tugged the journal out of her pocket. The mind map was folded neatly inside. She smoothed it out on the table and stared at it as if she were waiting for a message to appear. The musky dim was suddenly flooded with the late afternoon sunlight through the side door. A tall figure was silhouetted in the doorway. With a hearty hello to the bartender, he slid onto a barstool and ordered a drink. Molly realized she was tense. She just wanted to sit undisturbed. Hopefully he didn't notice her sitting in the corner. He took a long sip of his beer and looked at his phone. When she looked at him again, he was answering a call.

The door swung open again and two younger men entered, calling the bartender by name. Molly realized it was quitting time and the bar was starting to fill with the after work crowd. The sun nearly blinded her every time the door opened. Annoyed, she moved to another table where she felt hidden behind a pillar, but still see the door.

Molly thumbed through her journal while she nursed her drink. She looked around, it was all men. Definitely not a girly bar, she thought – so much for blending in.

She read back over her notes. *"Being able to listen and being perceived as a good listener are important leadership skills. Note that one must not only listen well but also be recognized as a good listener. So how do you do that?*

1. Stop anything else you are doing when someone is speaking to you. Multitasking doesn't work, and it is rude.

2. Ask questions based on what the person said.

3. Pay attention to non-verbal signals, body language, facial expressions, changes in tone of voice, vocal speed, nervous signs, or use of fillers.

4. Respond to attitude not just the words. For example, 'It sounds like this was a more challenging experience than normal. Can you tell me more so I can understand better?'

5. Summarize all sides of a disagreement equally and check whether you got it right before moving on.

6. Do pros and cons of suggested solutions, yours and others.

7. Get others' ideas on the table before you express any of yours so as not to influence.

8. Make it clear when you (or someone else) have to make the final decision, that all the input and ideas are important and need to be heard before the decision will be made. Once the decision is made, you will be asking for support so that it succeeds no matter which side they were on in the beginning."

A familiar voice broke her concentration, it was Daniel talking to the man at the bar. What the heck is he doing here, she wondered while pressing her back against the booth seat. Surely he didn't see her, she thought. How can she get out without being seen?

Daniel shook Gary's hand and hugged him with the other. Gary looked tanned and rested, completely opposite of how Daniel felt.

"Buddy, you are looking rough," Gary said.

"I'm pulled so many directions at the moment, it's starting to get to me," Daniel replied. "CeeCee and I are going in opposite directions, the kids are so busy with school that I never see them, and then there is all this business with the drug trial and the information leak. On top of all that, all that! I was invited to apply for the Trident Think Tank."

"Let me buy you a drink and we'll address all these problems," Gary said as he motioned to the bartender. "First, congratulations on the Trident nomination. I've heard nothing but good things about the entire process. As for you and CeeCee, it's time to decide if you are in or out. She's a good woman, but like anything worth pursuing, you can't leave it on autopilot."

"I know, I've been so preoccupied with the company that I hoped that it would just stay in holding mode until I could focus on the marriage once things at work calmed down."

Gary scowled.

"Let's talk about you first," Daniel interrupted. "Tell me how you do it, you look great. What are you doing down here playing golf?"

"I'm working on a merger deal," Gary replied.

"How do you do it? You have several businesses going but I never see you stressed out or overburdened. Clearly I'm floundering just running one," Daniel sighed.

"Danny boy, cut yourself some slack. You are smarter than you give yourself credit for. It's easy to beat up on yourself when things start to pile on top of each other. Look at all you've accomplished; you have a drug nearly ready for the market, you are known as one of the up and coming CEO power players in the industry and your employee retention rate is far above industry average, so you are doing something right. You rose to the challenge when the reins of the company were thrust in your hands," Gary replied.

"Thanks, I tend to forget that sometimes, I guess it's a confidence issue. I know my decision making process is different from my dad's, but he is still a very powerful force at Wilson-Shaw. I hope the Trident program will help me with some new skills that I can articulate back to Harold. I skimmed through the application, it will take some time and thought to complete it."

"That's part of the process," Gary nodded. "Thinking through your current situation helps establish a starting point so you and your mentor can focus on what you need to strengthen. Don't be surprised if you don't spend a lot of time on what you already do well."

"It seems you know a lot about it, did you do the program?" Daniel asked.

"I've been involved in various aspects from time to time, and I know some others who have been in the program. Speaking of Harold, how is your dad holding up?" Gary asked.

"I think he is glad to be busy and part of the company again. He said something earlier today that surprised me, that I was doing a good job handling things. He's never said that before," Daniel mused.

"Every time I've ran into him, he's been very vocal about how proud of you he is. It may be that he can't say it in front of you," Gary said.

"Yes, that whole praise in public and criticize in private mantra isn't part of his style," Daniel growled. "I know my identity isn't completely tied to my father's opinion of me, for chrissakes, I'm a grown man. But his comment today did take me by surprise."

"Let's talk about that," Gary continued. "What is the biggest issue you are facing at the moment?"

"Definitely the leak and the precarious swing in company value, I believe they are tied together. When word leaked that that actress was taking the drug, values shot up, then when she said it ruined her skin and hair, we nearly tanked. Harold wanted me to personally make a statement, however, I disagreed, saying the company as a whole should be represented and that our Public Affairs people could handle it. That's when he said he agreed with me and that I was doing a good job."

"What if there were more than one solution?" Gary asked.

"Isn't it obvious?" Daniel asked.

"Not always. You know, when I was a kid, I was hooked on Sherlock Holmes stories, actually any mystery story. The formula was fairly simple, you had the sidekick pointing out the obvious, while the hero took the time to pick up on other clues that many people miss. I just use that same philosophy in making business decisions, even in everyday life. Think of it as tool to be more open to solutions, really creative solutions and ideas if you just know how to set yourself up for it."

"So how does that apply to running a company?" Daniel asked.

"Start by reminding yourself that there is more than one possible solution."

"I think I do that—I'm always asking for everyone's ideas, to get a true range of input," Daniel interrupted.

"Diversity for its own sake doesn't ensure great ideas, just more ideas. More ideas allow for more good ideas to flow to the top. But just idea generation won't run a business," Gary continued. "Give yourself time for your brain to mull things over. What do you do when you have to think things over?"

"I hit the treadmill or the racquetball court, I need to move," Daniel asked.

Gary nodded, "Good strategy. So many people try to think things through but spend time working on another project. It's vital to avoid multitasking when you are up against a major project or problem. Focus on what is important, that means listening with full attention and observing, really seeing."

"I'm getting better at that, but it's a good reminder," Daniel agreed.

"The biggest impediment to learning anything is when you think you already know the answer. When someone closes their mind to new ideas because they think they know the solution they are already thinking about what they are going to say instead of listening to the other ideas," Gary went on. "This can even happen in your own mind when you decide you are done thinking about a subject because you have an answer. If you think there is only one answer—yours—then you have closed down your mind.

Even data that you are analyzing. Too often we read into or out of the data what we already believe. In a sense, we torture the data until it says what you want it to say."

"I'm guilty of that, I suppose most people in leadership positions are. But aren't we supposed to be tenacious, you know, stick to our goals?" Daniel asked.

"Being tenacious is good, being stubborn is not. Listening and questioning are skills, yet most of us grow up being taught not to question, especially those in authority. How is healthy skepticism to become part of a normal discussion? Didactic expression, to which there must be automatic acceptance is dangerous in life and business," Gary sipped his beer and fidgeted with the napkin. "Whenever I've questioned the acceptance of what is written in an article or trade journal, I am looked at as if I don't understand. People call me a trouble maker, when all I'm doing is asking questions to stimulate more discussion and new ideas."

"I remember Harold saying that about you when we first met, he said, 'Watch that guy, he seems to like to stir things up,'" Daniel laughed.

"Well, if that is my reputation, then I'll take it. There's no harm in stirring things up, it's when we leave it as the status quo that we stop innovating and growing," Gary added.

"But can't you have too many ideas? You know, analysis paralysis?"

"For all problem-solving in business it is best to come up with as many options to be considered as possible before making decisions. Large numbers of options does not mean analysis paralysis. This is a quick and useful method for looking at many sides of a situation and be sure it is understood before jumping to a conclusion."

Molly strained to hear the conversation between Gary and Daniel. Gary's voice carried over the other voices in the bar. The bartender had motioned to her a couple times asking about a refill, but she waved him off. Hopefully the men would go through the other door to the dining room, then she could make her way out the side door. She'd have to figure out something else for dinner. Of all places, how did he end up here she wondered.

"This is helpful Gary, thank you." Daniel said as he polished off the last of his beer. "Let me buy you a steak," he said as he slapped Gary on the shoulder. Daniel felt his phone vibrate in his pocket. It was a text message from Brooke. They located Molly's cell signal along a five mile stretch of route 234 near St. Mornay Beach.

"Holy crap," Daniel exclaimed.

"What?"

"My missing assistant is somewhere near here," Daniel replied.

"Your missing assistant? What do you mean?" Gary asked.

"Molly, my assistant, hasn't shown up for work for the past two days. She was handling the press releases and everything for the drug. It's not like her, she never misses, is always available even on the weekends, and the one time she was too sick to show up, she still worked from home. Now, no one can reach her. This text says she is within five miles of here."

Molly shrunk down in the booth. The air was suddenly heavy and hot. She could hear her heart beating in her ears. She could walk over and talk to them, or hide here and hope they didn't see her. She wasn't ready to talk to him, she certainly didn't mean for him to find her. She never considered this as a possibility. How did they find her? Damn cell phone, she thought. Even though she didn't take any calls, she listened to some of the voice mails which must have pinged the nearest tower. She remembered a missing teenager was located that way a few months ago. Did the company call the cops already? What if the cops are involved? She strained to see around the pillar to what Daniel was doing. He was still looking at his phone. She looked over toward the door, it was in direct sight of the bar and the bartender; they would see her exit.

Gary was looking at Daniel. "What are you thinking?" he asked.

"Something doesn't feel right. Suddenly I feel…odd. This is so strange. What would Molly be doing in this area? Why am I here too?"

"I don't know how you are going to find someone in a five mile radius," Gary said. "How do you know she's here?"

"We put the IT department on it, my CFO mentioned something about having her cell signal traced."

Molly froze. They *are* looking for me, she thought. She peered around the pillar again. Daniel's back was to her. Gary was busy looking at Daniel. There wasn't a chance that she could get through the door without being noticed.

Calm down, she told herself. Deep breath, just wait and see what he does.

"Try to call her again, maybe she'll pick up," Gary urged.

Molly grabbed at her hoodie pockets, then remembered she left her phone in the motel room.

"Let's get that steak, then I'll drive back tonight," Daniel said. "If she's in trouble, she would have let me know, I think she doesn't want to be found.

I thought she said something about visiting family, but I can't remember exactly. I was pretty wrapped up in some other things that day."

Gary tossed a $20 on the bar and nodded to the bartender. They went through to the other side of the bar into the restaurant. As she watched the door close behind Gary, Molly let out a sigh of relief. She grabbed her journal and headed for the side door.

"Come back again," the bartender called after her. It was just before sunset and the light was fading as she scooted across the street toward the motel. Slow down, look normal, she thought. She already realized that she would need to pack up and go – they were on her trail, if not the cops, the company was.

She cut across the parking lot next to the motel just as a shiny red SUV with extra lights across the back pulled in. That looks just like Brad's car, she thought. She did a double take looking at the driver, it was Brad.

She wheeled around and headed for the pool side entrance. Even though the pool was closed, the door still worked with a room key. She needed to get to her room, grab her things and get to her car before Brad could get to the front desk.

The gate by the pool was rusty and creaked as she swung it open. She kept her eye on the door, hoping she could get in. She was losing precious seconds fumbling in her pockets for the key. At last, she found it and shoved it in the electronic slot – it didn't light up. She tried again, nothing. Suddenly she heard shrieking voices on the other side. Molly jumped back as the door flung open and the two little boys from the beach burst through. The little boys were wide-eyed; Molly was too. She suddenly regained her composure and walked through the open door. The boy's mother was scurrying down the hall. She looked directly at Molly, recognizing her from the beach.

"They are still full of energy," she chuckled.

Molly nodded and smiled, hurrying down the hall to her room. She had to pass the opening that led to the lobby—Brad wasn't there. Perhaps he was still sitting in his vehicle or circling the lot looking for her car.

She slipped the key card into the lock and entered her darkened room. She slung her laptop bag over her shoulder with one hand while yanking the clothes off the hangers with the other. She stuffed the clothes into her bag and went over to the sink. Dragging her arm across the bathroom counter, she scooped her makeup directly into her bag. With both hands full, she looked around the room. It was difficult to see with just the light from the streetlamp. She flipped on the room light with her elbow, it looked like she had everything. Now to sneak out and get in the car before Brad got to the desk clerk. She hoped he was as pokey with Brad as he was when she checked in.

Bonus Stuff: There are many elements that affect levels of confidence. One has to do with style differences. For example, A quadrant (blue) people, make quick decisions. They might sometimes say, "Any decision is better than no decision." If they are approached later about new information and the necessity to change the decision, they are likely to be fine with the change. On the other hand, B quadrant (green) people, make careful, methodical decisions. They take their time and when they finally make a decision, they feel so confident and invested in their decision that they will become defensive if you tell them it was wrong. C quadrant (red) people, will consult their team before making a decision. If you later tell them there is new data and the decision needs to be changed, their reaction is likely to immediately go back and discuss it with the team, not just accept the change. D quadrant (yellow) make their decisions based on the big picture, their vision for future results. When told that new data means a change in the decision, they are ready to jump in to make the change. Change for D quadrant is interesting and fun and makes life more exciting.

11 BACK STEP

Daniel rolled over and tried to focus on the alarm clock—4:39. He rolled back over and closed his eyes. He felt CeeCee stirring beside him.

"You awake?" she asked softly.

"Yes, I didn't mean to bother you," he answered.

CeeCee rolled over to face him. "I missed you last night. I fell asleep just before midnight and you weren't home yet."

"I had dinner with Gary Brownlee, remember him? I needed to bounce some things off him. I didn't get a chance to tell you yet, but I was invited to apply for the Trident Think Tank."

"Really? Honey that's great," she replied.

"I wonder if this is really the best time to get into that, with this whole thing with the drug trial and that Meyers girl. Molly has been out of touch for the past two days, and what's weird, is that I met Gary in St. Mornay last night. The IT department said Molly's cell phone signal was picked up close to there."

"Her what? Cell phone signal? Isn't that illegal?"

"Not completely, it's a company issued cell phone, according to the legal department. It's just that of all the places to go, why would she be there?"

"What are you doing to find her?" CeeCee sat up in bed and smoothed the blankets.

"Security and IT are on it. It's not like her to disappear, I thought she had asked me to approve some time off to visit family, but I can't remember the conversation exactly. It was like she just threw that in while we were working on something else. That's what I can't remember."

"Well, in the meantime, I wouldn't pass on the Trident thing if I were you. There are some very big names that have come out of that program," CeeCee said.

"How do you know so much about it?"

"I did an article for Inside Business several months ago. The CEO of a fabrication company had just completed a year in the program and he said it was one of the best things he could have ever done to expand his thinking and decision making ability. I know you are an incredibly smart man already, but don't pass this up honey," CeeCee said softly.

Daniel kissed her forehead. "I won't. In fact, I want to get in early this morning and work on the application before anyone else gets in. Hey, let's plan to have a nice quiet dinner tonight. Want to go to 10 West?"

"I'd love it. The kids both have things going on after school, let's shoot for 6:30." She smiled.

Daniel was the first one into the executive parking lot. The sky was still dark with some lingering rain clouds. It felt out of sync starting the day at the office instead of the gym, but he decided he would work out once he had things well in hand. Gary's comments about considering other solutions, not just stopping at the first one, was still on his mind. The direct reports meeting would be a perfect environment to test it out. He also hoped the weather would be nice enough to have a stand up meeting in the courtyard again.

He opened his planner and started a list:

Think tank application

Molly's absence

Direct report meeting

Drug leak

Dinner with CeeCee

That should do it, he thought. Now he could focus on the application.

What types of thinking tools do you personally use?

What types of thinking tools do you advocate in working groups?

How do you choose working groups?

How do you reward collaboration?

What is your philosophy regarding project failure?

How often do you seek inspiration, collaboration or guidance from a source outside your industry?

How many books do you read per week/month/year?

What is your definition of a Brainiant company culture?

How would you describe your corporate culture?

What recent event or activity are you proud of?

What area do you struggle with?

Do you prefer to multi-task or concentrate on one issue at a time?

He realized this would take a while, but he was at least early enough to work on this for a solid hour without interruptions. He picked up the remote and turned on a CD, Bach with a contemporary twist. Nice background music for concentration.

What types of thinking tools do you personally use? Daniel hesitated for a moment. He wondered if running on a treadmill counted as a thinking tool. It helped him sort things out, it helped to keep his body moving while his mind turned things over. He kept lists, putting things to think about later in his paper parking lot. He wondered if the correct answer was brainstorming. He did that with his groups and direct reports, but it wasn't his first choice when he needed to make personal decisions.

What types of thinking tools do you advocate in working groups? Brainstorming was his usual method, although he recognized that it didn't always result in the best solution. Often the strong personalities in the room drowned out the quieter ones. Many of the research team members were not inclined to assert themselves in those types of environments, but later, they would submit ideas in writing which were truly exceptional.

The next question—*How do you choose working groups?* Caught him off guard. He wasn't really the one choosing the work group members, it was something he left to his direct reports. Was that something a CEO should influence? Maybe that tied into the corporate culture. He knew they were all struggling in that area. He was still trying to turn the tide on the old guard culture that his dad had created. He hoped the Trident program would help him in that area.

He reviewed the answer he had drafted the day before: Describe your current leadership style and how you would like to change or improve it.

I strive to maximize the effectiveness of my team, however, I am not always confident that I encourage them to succeed. Since many of my colleagues are my peers, I sometimes over-think my ability to be in charge. I know they are extremely skilled in their respective areas. However, I do feel that I am able to motivate others to contribute and engage authentically and I reinforce the value of our collective energy as a team.

The response sounded better than he remembered. He answered a few of the other questions and noticed Brooke standing at his office door.

"No offense, but I was hoping I wouldn't see you first thing this morning," Daniel said.

"I'm surprised too. I've sent Molly more texts, I've tried calling but it says her voice mailbox is full. What's going on with her? Should we be calling the police? Her family? Am I the only one that's worried?" Brooke asked.

"We know she is down south, somewhere around St. Mornay. I don't know why, but that's where the IT guys said she was. Which was very strange, I met Gary Brownlee in that very area yesterday. It was late and dark, so I didn't drive around. Molly is a smart gal, I'm not too worried about her safety, but I am concerned that mentally she may have hit a rough patch," Daniel said.

"That's all?" Brooke "A rough patch?"

"Brooke, I sense that you know something I don't, or else you wouldn't be so upset about this. What is it?" Daniel asked.

"I don't know more than you do, it's just that I when I was in college, a girl in my dorm disappeared. Everyone thought she was under the strain of finals and that she needed to get away. No one could reach her, everyone thought someone else was following up, and then," Brooke's voice quavered.

"They found her dead near a pond. Someone had attacked her."

Daniel stood up and came around the desk, he squeezed her forearm. "I'm sorry Brooke, perhaps I haven't been as concerned about Molly as I should be. I'll call down to HR and see who her emergency contacts are and get in touch with them."

"No need." Brooke and Daniel looked at each other in surprise. Brad was standing in the doorway.

"Why is that?" Daniel asked.

"I checked on it yesterday, the name on the paperwork was Melanie Meyers, it says she is a relative," Brad answered, shaking his head in disbelief. "I think we know now why she is not around, she must have leaked the info about the trial to Melanie or pulled some strings to get her into the trial."

"How is she related to Melanie?" Daniel asked.

"Not sure, it just says "relative" under the relationship box.

"Was there a contact number?"

"Yes, but it is disconnected. She hasn't updated her personal information in over five years. There's no telling how old that number is." Brad replied.

Daniel looked at Brad. He felt a knot in his gut. He realized that the thing that bugged him about Brad was lack of eye contact. Brad rarely looked directly at Daniel. That was it, it always seemed that he was trying to avoid being direct or authentic. Brad was talking to the corner of the room, not directly to Daniel.

"Brad, the IT department sent me a message last night that they had picked up a signal from Molly's cell near St. Mornay last night. I just happened to be in St. Mornay. Don't you think that's a bit odd?" Daniel kept his gaze locked on Brad. Brad looked down at the floor.

"That sure does sound odd. Do we know if she knows anyone there?" Brad continued to talk to the floor.

"I think we should call the police, it's been three days," Brooke interrupted.

"No!" Brad looked up. "I mean, I don't think so at this point, we should just follow up on the signal ourselves. We have a security department, and if she is related to the same Melanie Meyers that is our drug trial leak, we need to have reasonable cause to call in the police first. I mean, the name Melanie

Meyers isn't all that unique – it could be a fluke."

Daniel looked at Brad, puzzled. "I'm not so sure. I think we have a legitimate concern about her safety at this point. As Brooke said, it's been three days. You can file a missing person report after 24 hours, clearly we are behind the curve here."

"What about us already tracing her cell phone signal? How do you presume to explain that to police?" Brad asked.

"Her cell is issued through the company, it is company property, right?" Daniel looked to both of them for agreement.

"Sounds right to me," Brooke nodded. "Please, let me call security and get started on this."

"They already know," Brad answered. He caught the look from Daniel. He held out his hands and for once, looked at Daniel directly. "Hey, our entire fiscal year, heck, the entire company is riding on the approval of RQ246. Security has been on the leak since it happened. As CFO, I have to protect the value of this company, it's pretty shaky right now. "

Daniel nodded. "I agree, however, it seems as though they should have discovered the connection to Melanie Meyers, the cell phone trace, all that. Evidently they didn't register the gravity of the situation."

"They know. They know," Brad huffed as he turned to leave the office.

"Where are you going? We need a clearer game plan here," Daniel said. "Brad, stay here. Brooke, call security and legal and get them in my office, pronto."

"On it," she said.

Brooke had already left the office when Daniel meekly added, "Please."

Bonus stuff: Brainiance® refers to a deep acceptance and understanding of different styles of thinking. A company with a Brainiant culture embraces the differences because it allows for creativity, option thinking, innovation, and better decisions.

Awareness of thinking style differences can be improved by assessments designed for that purpose such as disc, HBDI®, MINDEX®, and MBTI®. There are many different assessments available to help you determine your dominant thinking style cluster. Each of the assessments has some unique features, however they are all based originally on the ideas and research of the Swiss psychiatrist Karl Jung (1875-1961).

Personality styles affect decision making, acceptance of change, relationships, communication, and other interactions at work. Knowledge of the differences between the styles helps a business person approach work and relationships in a knowledgeable and helpful manner.

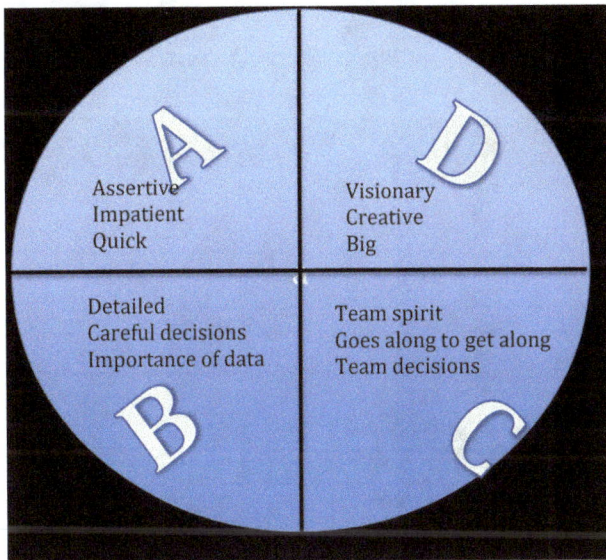

An organization that understands great ideas can come from any level not just management, gives everyone the chance to think of ways to make improvements, new products or services, or new methods.

Diversity of thinking styles means using all quadrants of our brain.

Some see ideas, some hear ideas, some feel ideas, some picture the future, some bring together people, some pull in the details, and some help the group focus on the bottom line. All can be encouraged to piggyback ideas on each other's ideas.

The combination makes a great team.

12 BLINDING SPEED

Molly woke to a knock on the car window. She squinted in the early morning sun and swept the hair off her face. All she could see was a blue shirt with a bright yellow SECURITY printed above the pocket. As she rolled down the window, the figure stepped back. He was tall, but on second look, he was also very young. He couldn't have been more than 20 years old.

"Ma'am. Are you ok? There is no overnight parking allowed here," he said softly.

"Yes, I just got a little drowsy driving last night, and I didn't know when I'd find a motel," Molly smoothed out her shirt and sat up straight.

"Well, it is smart to stop driving when you're tired, but like I said, we don't allow overnight parking. So, unless you are going to shop in the store, I'll have to ask you to leave."

"No problem, in fact, I was going to go in for a few things," Molly said. She looked around the parking lot, there were already several cars, but none that looked like Brad's. She zipped up her hoodie and pushed her wallet into her pocket. She kept looking around as she got out of the car.

"Are you looking for someone?" the security guard asked.

"No, oh no," Molly said. "I was just trying to get my bearings."

"You're on Route 234 and the big intersection is just ahead. You can catch Highway 1 there. You'll find some hotels there if you plan on staying in the area," he answered.

Molly stretched out her arms and raised up on her toes. She had only been asleep for a few hours but the car was certainly not one made for napping. She stretched again and walked toward the store doors, looking around for any vehicle that looked like the one she saw the night before. She was certain it was Brad's, she remembered seeing it in the parking lot one night when they left early due to a snow storm. She couldn't help but notice all the extra lights he had across the back of his SUV. But lots of people drove that same model, maybe the lights were not that unusual.

She thought back over the events of last night. It was all too close for comfort, what were the odds that her boss would show up in the same bar that she was trying to hide out in? He must have already known where she was before getting the message about the cell phone signal. She had turned it off and taken out the battery once she was on the road last night. She just wanted to get out of there and get some distance between her and St. Mornay.

She entered the store and picked up a shopping basket. She picked out a couple of apples, bananas, a turkey sandwich, and a small bottle of orange juice. She caught a whiff of the freshly baked bread in the bakery and her stomach growled. She didn't eat dinner last night since she had to flee the bar. By the time she got to the checkout, her basket was nearly overflowing: bagels, cheese, yogurt, and some other goodies had made it into her basket. It wouldn't go to waste, she planned to stay out of sight as much as possible. She would have to find another hotel room and stay put. As she was checking out, she saw pre-paid phone cards and added one to the pile of groceries. She counted her cash, she knew she couldn't use her credit card anymore – that was traceable. It's time to get creative, she thought.

"Someone got hungry," The cashier said as she scanned the items.

"What else do people buy food for?" Molly snapped.

"Sorry, I just noticed you when I came into work this morning. I've had to do that, you know, live out of my car. It's not exactly glamorous."

Molly felt embarrassed for snapping at the cashier. "I'm not really living out of my car, just driving through, I got a little too sleepy last night and didn't see any hotels, so I pulled in to sleep for a bit."

"If you need a place to shower and clean up, you can get a day pass at the Fitness Express across the street, it's only $7.50. I did that a lot when I didn't have anywhere else. Ron is the owner, he's cool with it. Tell him Angie sent you and he may knock it down to $5."

Molly smiled at the girl. She realized she wasn't more than 21. She couldn't imagine being homeless and trying to find ways to be creative about hygiene or details like that.

"How long have you worked here?" Molly asked.

"I've been here two years, I'll be in the management trainee program starting next month. If it weren't for this job, I would have really been in a jam. They never knew I was homeless, now that I'm back on my feet, things are falling into place, life is good."

"Thanks for the tip, and good luck, I'm sure you'll make a great manager. Molly scooped up her bags and headed toward the door.

She was still smiling as she walked to her car. The sun was bright, the air was crisp and a gentle breeze tossed her hair. She thought about the cashier's words, *life is good.* She wondered if the girl had ever felt panicked or hopeless. "I don't have anything to whine about, what the heck was I thinking?" she said aloud.

She couldn't decide what she needed first, a shower or something to eat. She pulled a banana off the top of the bag and began to peel it while she unlocked her car. It was delectable. It was as if she had never tasted a banana before, the creamy texture, the surge of sweetness. She savored the flavor on her tongue, concentrating on the moment. How many times had she gulped down her lunch, not even paying attention to what it tasted like? It always seemed like she was in a rush, never fully mindful of the moment. She knew it was just part of the job, but she wondered how effective she could be if given the flexibility to fully develop some of the ideas she had mentioned to Daniel.

She wondered what he was thinking about her absence. She could only hear snippets of the conversation between Daniel and Gary the night before. Gary seemed more concerned that he was missing an assistant than Daniel did, but that was his style, to downplay things in order to appear calm, when in fact he would be rattled on the inside. She wondered what he would think when he realized what she had done.

She shook her head, trying to come back to reality. She plucked the turkey sandwich from the bag and unwrapped it. She stopped, closed her eyes and concentrated on the smell. She took a bite and felt a rush on her taste buds. Was it just because she was so hungry or paying closer attention, she wondered. Eating the sandwich and the banana had turned into a pleasant, mindful experience.

She rolled up the wrapping and the napkin and stuffed it back into the sack. Digging in the back seat, she opened her bag and rummaged through, looking for some clean underwear. She felt gritty from the walk on the beach and especially stale from sleeping in the car. She found some underwear, a clean shirt and her deodorant and rolled them together. She decided she could use the exercise and walked across the street to the gym.

She opened the door to a whirlwind of activity, the mom crowd had taken over the treadmills and elliptical machines, the morning talk shows blaring on the TV's mounted above. There was a tall man with long blond hair at the desk, he looked more like a surfer dude, but she figured it was Ron.

He smiled. She noticed that he looked down at her roll of clothes. He nodded as if it were ok to approach the desk.

"Can I help you?" he asked.

"Are you Ron?" she didn't wait for him to answer. "Angie across the street said you could help me out with a day pass. "

"Did you say Angie? In that case I do. Do you have a five?" he asked.

Molly fished the bill out of her pocket. "Thanks, I'm just driving through, got too tired last night and ended up sleeping in my car. I won't be long just need to freshen up."

"Hey, it's ok. We've all been there at one time or another." He handed her two fluffy white towels.

As noisy as the gym was, the locker room was quiet and nicer than most gyms she had been to.

She picked a stall and turned on the water, it was hot and steamy in a matter of seconds. She undressed and stepped in. Closing her eyes, she concentrated on feeling the water run down her back. Just like the accentuated taste of the banana, the shower seemed extraordinary. As soon as she noticed her mind wandering, she said "Stop" to herself and redirected her attention to the shower. She wanted to focus only on the sensations of the water, her fingers across her scalp, the foam of the shampoo. It had a subtle citrus scent. She rinsed and shampooed again. She was beginning to feel energized.

After she dried off and dressed, she realized she didn't have a comb. Running her fingers through her hair, she dried it a little with the hair dryer and decided she would fix it better in the car. She rolled up her dirty clothes, tossed the towels in the hamper and made her way to the exit. Ron was standing near a weight machine, giving an older man tips on an exercise.

She looked around the gym, everyone was scurrying through their workouts as if they had more important things to do. She was tired of hurrying, cramming so much into a day. She wondered if she were the only one who felt that way. As she turned to leave, Ron's voice startled her.

"Leaving so soon?"

"Well, I need to get on the road," Molly said.

"Where are you headed?" he asked.

Her heart raced, she didn't want to leave more of a trail than she already had, especially if Brad were on her tail, looking for her. "Crandall." She blurted.

"You're a bit off course aren't you?" Ron's eyes narrowed.

"I had another stop along the way. Hey, I really need to get going. Thanks for the day pass." Molly headed out the door.

"Crandall," she said to herself. Where did I come up with that? Maybe Crandall wasn't a bad idea, it was further inland and large enough she could blend in easily. If Brad were truly on her tail, he wouldn't think of Crandall since it required some back tracking, but she doubted it would be anyone's first guess. Hotels would be cheaper there too.

She darted across the street, scurrying to her car. She checked her hoodie pocket, no keys. She laid her dirty clothes on the hood of the car and searched her other pockets. No sign of them. She tried the car door, locked. She peered inside, there, hanging from the ignition were her keys. She pounded the window. "Damn!" She cried. So much for being mindful.

She looked around the parking lot for the security guard that had found her that morning. The lot was full of shoppers wheeling their carts filled with bags, no one seemed to notice her. She tried the door again.

The last thing she wanted to do was go back across the street and ask Ron for help. Something about him made her uneasy. She thought of Angie, the cashier. A former homeless person probably has a few other tricks up her sleeve, she thought.

She rolled the clothes up tight and set them in the gap between the hood and the windshield. Back inside the store, there were several lanes with shoppers checking out but no sign of Angie.

Damn again, Molly thought. She looked around, no sign of the security guard either. She approached the first cashier who was nearly flinging the items across the belt. The cashier looked up at Molly and scowled. Not her, Molly thought and walked down to the next cashier. She was at least smiling.

"I'm looking for Angie," Molly said.

"Angie? Angie who?" the cashier asked.

"She was on the first register earlier this morning," Molly said, pointing toward the entrance.

"Honey, I've been here for seven years, we don't have no Angie working here."

"An" Molly snipped.

"What?"

"You don't have *an* Angie working here." Molly said over her shoulder as she walked away.

This makes no sense, she thought. I talked to her, even Ron seemed to know Angie when I asked for the day pass. Maybe my mind is playing tricks on me.

She was almost out the door when the young security guard approached her. "You're still here?" he asked.

"Well, actually, I locked my keys in my car. I was all set to go. I did shop in the store, I wasn't sleeping again," she added hastily.

"I have a Slim Jim, I'll be right there," the young man smiled.

Molly was leaning against the car door as he approached with the metal strip. "You're lucky" he said as he walked up to her.

"How's locking one's keys in one's car considered lucky?" she asked.

"These older model cars aren't all electronic, so you can fish down along the side of the door mechanism and trip the lock," he said as he slid the strip along the window. "Hum, seems I missed it, sometimes it takes a few tries." He moved the strip over and slowly pushed it into the door again.

"Can I ask you something?" Molly asked.

"Sure, like did I receive special training for this?" he teased.

"Not exactly. It was just that I was in there this morning and the cashier that checked me told me to tell the guy at the gym that Angie sent me, but when I went in again to ask for her, I was told there was no Angie working there. Am I losing it?" Molly wondered.

The security guard froze.

"What did I say?" Molly asked.

"How do you know about Angie?" He turned and peered down at her. She realized he was almost a foot taller than her.

"Like I said, she waited on me this morning at the cash register."

He turned back to the car and shoved the Slim Jim down the side of the door, the lock popped open and he pulled on the handle.

"Here you go. I suggest you just get in and drive on like you said you would. I didn't see you here. I won't tell anyone you were here. Be safe, have a nice day."

Bonus Stuff: Everyone needs a way to organize, remember, prioritize information, and check assumptions. These days with all the smart phone applications and the ability to research any person's name or company, there is no reason to rely only on our memory, whether or not we have found it to be faulty at times.

In spite of how expansive all this data is for our thinking, we also need to remain skeptical enough to question whether what we think we heard or saw was accurate and complete; whether we missed something important or were distracted when we shouldn't have been; or whether we jumped to a conclusion without having enough evidence to come to that conclusion.

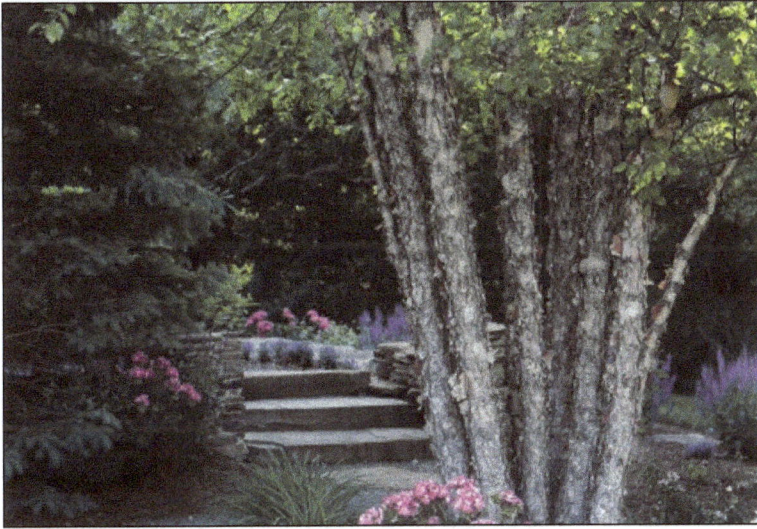

A Creativity Garden by Audrey Wancket, CPP Master Photographer

13 BUILDING SYNERGY

The mid-morning sun had warmed the courtyard and the leaves on the trees were just beginning to open. Daniel was happy to see several of the directors already milling around talking together.

"Good morning. Thank you for being prompt. I want to share some ideas with you and how I would like this to become part of our corporate culture. Last week I presented the idea of mixing up your working groups to get some new perspectives. Today, I'd like to take a few minutes to share some team decision making and creativity strategies with you."

He looked around and noticed that Brad was not in the group. "Is there anyone from Finance here? I don't see Brad." He asked.

The group looked around at each other. No one came forward. Daniel tried to hide his irritation. He and Brad had seemed out of sync since the drug trial scandal broke. Now he was missing a director's meeting. He closed his eyes for a moment and took a breath. *I don't need to worry about it right now*, he told himself.

Regaining his concentration, he continued. "Thank you for your dedication and expertise, we are making great strides as an organization. Creativity and problem solving has been our forte, otherwise, we wouldn't be this close to approval on a new, ground-breaking medication. What I want to avoid is falling into the same way of thinking, or as I call it the 'We've always done it this way' chorus." A wave of nervous chuckles swept over the group.

"What I envision for us is a culture that encourages creativity in our decision making process, being more open to alternatives that may be out of the mainstream. Going beyond the obvious answer to the what-if's that help us be far more innovative. Exploring what alternatives are available, what risks are associated with making a wrong or poor decision, what are the pros and cons of each of the alternatives, and do these align with company vision, mission, values and goals?"

Daniel looked over at the head of manufacturing. "Ed, what do you find to be the biggest obstacle to teamwork and decision making?"

Ed thought for a moment. "It would have to be thinking you already know the answer. When someone closes their mind to new ideas because they think they know the solution they are already thinking about what they are going to say instead of listening to the other ideas."

"I agree," came another voice from behind Ed. "This can even happen in your own mind when you decide you are done thinking about a subject because you have an answer. If you think there is only one answer, yours, then you have closed down your mind." Others nodded in agreement.

"Can you give me a specific situation?" Daniel asked.

Ed cleared his throat, "Sure, we had data showing our workflow and delivery times. Some of my foremen were trying to torture the data to get it to say what they wanted to say. Thinking that it reflected what they already believed. Once we stepped back and tried a different approach, we could see that it was not in line with what we thought was happening."

"Excellent example." Daniel said. Ed's face brightened.

"Now, I want you to take a task back to your departments," Daniel said. "The next time you are at a point to make a decision, long or short term, I'd like you to address it from a team building aspect. That means you need to have agreement, not just people nodding heads. A list of various alternatives and a consensus of which alternative has the most pros, least cons, and least risks. Asking for solutions – plural - will reinforce the belief that they can come up with multiple solutions, rather than stopping at one.

There will be a run-down of the pertinent points in the shared drive for all of you to review, and I want you to share it with your departments. The information is some that I had access to awhile back, but it was during a conversation last night that I was reminded of it. We are poised for another growth spurt as RQ246 hits the market. Other companies will want to buy us or take us over, and I'm not saying this to alarm anyone, but we need to have our next idea for our next product already in the wings and ready to follow the success of RQ246. I know we have the talent, resources and certainly the brain power."

As the meeting broke up, Daniel watched as the various department heads continued conversations. When they met in the board room, it seemed that everyone was closed off and in a hurry to get back to their offices. Out here, in the open, with sunshine, fresh air, and birds singing in the background, Daniel could see everyone was more open and engaged.

He went back up to his office where Brooke was waiting. She seemed nervous and more upset than before.

"They don't have a cell signal anymore. They haven't been able to track anything since the middle of last night."

Daniel sat down hard at his desk. He was beginning to realize how serious it was that Molly was missing.

"Brooke, how well do you know Molly?"

"Not all that well. We talk, we've had lunch together a few times, but she doesn't say much about her personal life."

"Has she ever said anything about family? A boyfriend?" Daniel asked.

"I would think that you would know if she has a boyfriend, after all, she is your assistant and from what I've seen, she is here late most of the time. I don't know of too many relationships that can handle lots of overtime at the office."

"Well, that's true," Daniel said as he looked at the ceiling.

"I didn't mean anything by that," Brooke added. "I'm not saying your relationship…well, I'm sorry, I better be quiet."

"No, it's no secret that I am not home with my wife and kids very much. Which reminds me, I did promise CeeCee dinner tonight at 10 West. I'll need to make a reservation."

"But what about Molly? I'm concerned, aren't you?" Brooke asked.

"Yes I am." Daniel leaned back in his chair and studied the ceiling again. "I know that Molly is highly dependable, so this type of disappearance is concerning. I also know that many times I don't pay as close attention to what she tells me as I should. She handles many details for me and I have never needed to micromanage her.

It seems that I remember her saying she had family visiting or was taking vacation or something. I just don't know why I can't remember. I didn't want to jump to conclusions at first because I thought that she had taken time off and I didn't remember it was this week. I also didn't get too worried because I could remember a conversation we had one time where she said that she'd love to just pack up and disappear for a day or two to clear her head. It was after Fred died in that hiking accident – she took a couple days off. She used to be his assistant before she was assigned to me. She took it hard and I remember her saying that it just helped to be away from things for a couple days. I wondered if that wasn't the case now. I've been overloading her with a dozen different projects."

"Maybe that's it. She just needed time away," Brooke tried to convince herself. "I can't help but think that something's not right, I can just feel it. I know that may sound strange, but I've found that listening to my gut is usually very reliable. It's like a sixth sense. That may sound silly but…"

"Not at all," Daniel interrupted. "I can appreciate the power of a hunch or a gut reaction. I rely on them too. One of the workshops I attended explained different thinking styles. One of them was feeling - which I think applies to me. I like to physically walk through a sequence to understand how it works instead of reading about it or listening to someone explain it. I also think that's why I run so much, I can sort things out while my body is busy doing something else."

Brooke was still standing in front of his desk, waiting for his answer about Molly.

"I'm sorry Brooke, I realize we haven't solved anything about Molly.

Honestly, I had hoped that security would have already located her and just found out if she were ok. I think the next step is to file a missing persons report."

"I asked about that, but the guy in security brushed that off," Brooke answered.

"I'll talk to him," Daniel said. "In the meantime, I have a file on creative team building and decision making. I'd like you to make a folder on the shared drive for it and put the summary sheet in there."

Brooke looked incredulous.

"I understand your concern Brooke, but we also have to keep things running – especially on the surface. We don't want people alarmed about Molly's absence, we don't need a lot of publicity about it either. The stockholders and board of directors are already making noise about the company valuation which they think is in jeopardy because of that actress. We continue to operate business as usual." Daniel declared.

He scrolled through the files on his computer, locating the handout on team decision making. He read over the document:

1. The problem or purpose must have agreement. This takes more than just nodding heads when you state the purpose. There must be agreement on what the words mean in describing the project, and everyone must feel that they mutually own the problem and are part of the solution.

2. They need to feel accountability to each of the members of the team not just to the problem or leader.

3. They need to discuss and agree on process. How will they share the work? How will they keep each other informed? How will decisions be made and re-visited if necessary? How urgent are the parts or the whole of the problem? Differing senses of urgency can undermine the project.

4. How will they decide when the project is finished and how will everyone enjoy the fruits of the labor? It could be a celebration or an announcement or other incentive.

Daniel saved the file and dropped it in the shared file while copying Brooke. "Here's the first file, I will probably add a couple more," he called from his office.

Another title caught his eye. *Is Criticism Ever Constructive?"* He skimmed over the copy, *How do you answer when someone asks, "Would you like some constructive criticism?"*

Even more important, how do you feel when asked that question? Most of us will cringe on the inside. The dominant word in that question is criticism. Constructive or not (and that is often in the eye of the beholder) you prepare yourself for something negative. You may even subconsciously prepare to defend yourself even before you hear what the criticism will be.

Daniel thought back to the time his dad first offered his constructive criticism. Daniel had prepared a presentation for his high school debate team and delivered it flawlessly to him in the living room. Harold listened intently, then sat quietly for a moment after Daniel had finished.

"Son, let me offer you some constructive criticism."

Daniel remembered the punch to his gut, the pounding of his heart, so loud he couldn't hear what his Dad was saying. All he remembered was Harold's disapproving tone. Once Harold saw that Daniel was crushed, he only added, "Get used to it son, if you are going to survive in the business world, you'll have to take the lumps as well as the rewards."

Daniel chuckled to himself. I guess things haven't changed much, he thought. He read on:

How you receive the criticism can make a difference in how your relationship continues. If the information does turn out to be very helpful and you will use it, say thank you. You may even want to say thank you for taking the time to tell you with the risk of not knowing how you will take the criticism.

Now, how about when the tables are turned and you are feeling compelled to give constructive criticism? Think first whether giving the feedback will be appreciated and make a difference. Some issues are too trivial to take that risk.

If the suggestion will help your coworker and it is a large enough issue to address, then whatever you say has to come across as supportive and caring, and most of all, respectful. That doesn't mean that you have to apologize for giving feedback. If you make too big a deal, your coworker may feel you have a hidden agenda. Successful feedback must feel like collaboration, even if you are the boss.

Daniel wished that he and Harold had been better at collaborating, rather than Harold bossing Daniel. He respected his dad's experience, it was just difficult to be open to Harold barking orders, rather than helping him learn to think things through. The only time he did appreciate his dad looking over his shoulder was when they were talking money. Harold had a keen grasp on the overall picture.

Daniel's reminder alarm buzzed—Brad and Harold were due in a few minutes to go over the latest financial position. He quickly saved the file and added it to the shared drive.

He could hear Harold's voice outside his office, he was talking to Brooke. He usually joked around with the assistants, but their conversation was hushed. Daniel was straining to hear what was going on. Then he heard Brad's voice too. He got up and met them at the door.

"I missed you in the direct reports meeting this morning," Daniel said as Brad took a seat in front of Daniel's desk.

"I had my hands full, these numbers are not going to make you feel good," Brad sighed as he leaned forward and laid out three spreadsheets on Daniel's desk. Brad was talking quickly, jumping from one page to the next, then back again. Daniel wasn't concentrating on the numbers as much as he was trying to study Brad; his voice seemed thin and wispy, he kept his eyes on the papers and kept talking, leaving no room for Daniel to ask a question.

"Brad. Dude, slow down. Bottom line, what does all this mean?" Daniel struggled to contain his frustration.

"Red, it means we are in the red. If the second quarter is like the first, we are heading for a major decrease in stock values. I'm sure you understand," Brad's voice turned icy. "Why don't you explain what's happening?"

Daniel looked directly at Brad. The two were locked in a stare down. Harold was unusually still, then cleared his throat and shifted in his chair. "Gentlemen, this is obviously a tense situation, however…"

Brad snapped his finger toward Harold. "I believe Daniel knows exactly why we are in the position we are in, as CEO, there is no way he would be leaving anything to chance—or to anyone else, unless it was all part of his overall plan," he said, holding his stare with Daniel.

"What plan are you insinuating?" Daniel shot back.

"The plan to manipulate the drug trial to cause us to lose nearly half our value. His Hollywood stunt," Brad sneered.

"What the hell are you talking about?" Daniel's mouth went dry. Brad didn't blink. "I said, what the hell are you talking about?"

Brad's shoulders relaxed as he looked at Daniel, then slowly over to Harold, then back to Daniel's stare. "Security discovered that the Melanie

Meyers listed as your assistant's emergency contact is in fact, the Melanie Meyers in Hollywood. Clearly they conspired to concoct this Hollywood scandal. This explains Molly's unauthorized absence and silence. She is obviously part of this, her cell signal is no longer traceable. Both she and Daniel were in St. Mornay at the same time. There is ample evidence of collusion."

"Bullshit!" Daniel jumped from his chair. "That's absolute bullshit."

"Danny, calm down," Harold was standing beside him. He turned to Brad, "You better have absolute evidence of the allegation you are making. This company has always been run with full integrity and transparency. We have no reason to manipulate anything, especially the results of a drug that will help thousands of people, not to mention the millions of dollars it will generate—all of which turns right around into research and development of more life-saving drugs and devices. If you are going to raise such an accusation, you accuse us both," Harold boomed.

"I'm doing you a favor," Brad retorted. "The board of directors is gathering later today for a vote of no-confidence. You have time to get an attorney and tender your resignation. I highly suggest you do so, and be sure he's a criminal attorney, because as the evidence comes out, I'm sure you'll be appearing before a grand jury."

The room was stifling—Daniel's heart was racing. "What the hell?"

Harold leaned over the desk and glared at Brad. "Mr. Davis, this meeting is adjourned."

Brad's held his icy stare as he gathered up the spreadsheets and stood up.

"Leave the documents," Harold ordered.

"I don't believe that is an option," Brad replied.

"Leave them," Harold growled. Brad slowly laid the papers back on the desk and backed away.

Bonus Stuff: Do you remember debate teams from high school or college? An issue was assigned and each team told what position hey had to argue. That meant that they had to do research and develop the argument for the side they were given, not the side they might have intuitively chosen.

When a decision needs to be made and is important it may be time to set up two (or more if there are more than two viewpoints to consider) teams who are told they need to develop a strong case for the side they have been assigned.

Because the 'sides' are assigned, follow up discussions focus on the issues and not the messenger.

14 BRACE YOUR SELF

Daniel looked out his office window to the courtyard below. A small group in lab coats were standing there talking. He chuckled at the irony. One of the lab departments had adopted the outdoor meeting idea, while he stood here, waiting for lead company counsel.

"Danny, before Vaughn gets here, is there anything you want to tell me?" Harold asked.

"No Dad, this is all a load of crap." Daniel turned around. "My work with Molly has always been above board. I am not manipulating anything."

"Well son, Brooke tells me you weren't very concerned about Molly, you weren't doing much to locate her. I'm just not sure why that is, unless the two of you were in some sort of contact."

"Dad, again. I am not in any sort of scheme with Molly. I never knew she had a sister, let alone one that is a Hollywood actress. It has never, ever come up in conversation," Daniel's index finger pounded the spreadsheets.

"This just can't be right, how in the world would there be any way for Molly's sister to get that drug? How would Molly have the connections to get her into the trial? If that is the case, we could be in serious legal trouble if the study is not blind. It's just too coincidental, I know. But if she were smart enough to circumvent the protocol, then there are more company secrets in jeopardy."

"You better hope its only coincidence. I'm telling you at the moment, things don't look good," Harold sighed.

Brooke knocked at the door. "He's here," she whispered.

Harold and Daniel both nodded as Vaughn entered the room, the door clicking heavily behind him.

"Daniel, we have a very serious situation here. My office has been notified that there is a potential action by the board of directors this afternoon. It is a confidence vote, and with the evidence presented, it appears that this will end poorly," Vaughn said.

"What evidence?" Daniel was incredulous.

"My office determined the evidence gathered by both the IT and Security departments would substantiate a collusive act between you and your assistant," Vaughn said.

"I would like to see this evidence," Harold said.

"As would I," said Daniel.

"Your attorney will have to request it," Vaughn said.

"My attorney? You are my corporate counsel." Daniel countered.

"I'm sorry Mr. Shaw, in this case, I cannot represent you. This involves your personal actions and how it affects the company. I can only represent Wilson-Shaw as a company," Vaughn said.

Daniel thought he looked slightly pleased to deliver the news. He looked over at Harold, who was shaking his head and looking at his hands. "Dad? What am I supposed to do?" Daniel asked. "My own IT and Security departments are pointing the finger at me. I have no idea where Molly is or why she hasn't shown up to work. If in fact Melanie Meyers is her sister, her connection to the drug trial is completely new to me."

"How do you answer for the two of you being in St. Mornay at the same time?" Vaughn quizzed.

"I was meeting with Gary Brownlee, a personal friend of mine. I wasn't aware she was in the same town until I received a text from the IT department that they detected Molly's cell signal near there. Pure coincidence. Gary was sitting right there with me at dinner when I received the text," Daniel said.

"I suggest you save that for your testimony," Vaughn said. "You should stop talking to me and start engaging counsel. I would suggest Archer, Bergland and Marlow. That is the extent of advice I can provide to you." He arose from his seat and nodded. As Vaughn left the room, Daniel felt a wave of nausea come over him.

"This is not the time to fold," Harold said.

"I'm not going to fold," Daniel said determinedly. "This has all the makings of a set-up. Wilson-Shaw is poised for exponential growth. The approval of RQ246 will raise us to global stature, our research will be world renowned. There is absolutely no reason to throw a monkey wrench into that. What do you know about Archer, Bergland and Marlow? Have you heard of them before?"

Harold shook his head. "I know Marlow personally, the other two I only know of. I think he is a complete sleaze. That could serve us well or it could ruin us."

"I don't need a sleaze for a lawyer. If I were guilty, then maybe. I need someone who will believe me when I say that I am not involved in any such behavior," Daniel said.

"It's past that now, if you've been accused and they have any sort of evidence, even circumstantial, you are on the defensive." Harold sighed.

"If they vote no-confidence, then I'm out?" Daniel asked.

"Not completely, but it could lead to a further action to remove you."

"I have a call to make," Daniel picked up his cell phone. As he started to dial, he touched the keypad on his computer—the screen was blue. He clicked the mouse. Still blue. "Brooke," he called "I'm locked out, call IT."

"Danny, son, IT locked you out. Your hands are tied until the vote," Harold said softly. Before he could respond, there was a voice at the other end of his cell.

"Danny boy!" Gary sounded as chipper as ever.

"Gary, I've got a shit storm brewing, I need your help." Daniel said.

"You've got it brother, what's happening?"

Daniel relayed the morning's events. Gary sighed. "This is the wildest thing I've ever heard. Danny, I know you, and I know this isn't how you do business. This is no time for playing nice. I know an attorney—he's big money, but you are looking at jail time if you lose. Give me just a few minutes to make a call and bring him up to speed. I'll call you right back. Hang in there."

As the call ended Daniel pushed #2 on his phone. He needed to tell CeeCee. After a couple rings, he realized it would go to her voice mail. He hung up and dialed the house phone, again, it continued to ring. "Come on," he muttered.

He felt a hand on his back. CeeCee was there. He dropped the phone and gathered her up in his arms. She felt smaller than he remembered. The distance between them seemed to melt away. He felt her clinging to him just as desperately.

"Sweetheart, your father called me. I don't understand what all this is about, but I'm here. Just tell me what I can do to help," she whispered. Daniel buried his head into her hair and held on. He wasn't sure what to do.

"Greg Brownlee is calling me with an introduction to a lawyer. This is coming out of our pockets, the company can't protect me. CeeCee, this could wipe us out. The kids' college…the house…it could be…"

"Shh," she said. "Why make money if we can't use it when we need it? Right now we need to tackle this. The house, the kids, we'll all be fine. It's time to circle the wagons and face this together," she said.

The cell buzzed, "Here's the call," Daniel said as he scrambled for the phone.

CeeCee stood nearby while Daniel answered a few questions and then fell silent.

"Uh-huh," Daniel said. "Yes, yes sir," and began to jot down notes. He said goodbye and hung up the phone.

"Well?" CeeCee asked.

"I have a meeting with him later today. He says for now to stay in the office and proceed as normally as possible. Locking me out of my computer access isn't illegal, but he says to just play it cool. He'll be here by the time the board meets," Daniel answered.

"Did he say if they could fire you outright?" CeeCee asked.

"Maybe, but he thinks it's more of a no-confidence vote, just to send me a message. If I haven't had issues with the board before, it's not likely to go from a good relationship to firing me just like that. Although he says the allegations are serious, if I have leaked industry secrets, then I may have no recourse."

"But you've done no such thing!" CeeCee wept.

"You and I know that, but at the moment, we are the only two," Daniel answered. "I think I've got a tough road ahead. I'm being squeezed, pure and simple."

"Who is the lawyer?"

"Weiss, can you believe that? J.T. Weiss. I don't know whether to laugh or cry," Daniel shook his head. "Where did Dad go? He's got to hear this."

"He was on his phone in the hallway when I came in," CeeCee said. "I'll go see if I can find him."

Daniel leaned back in his chair and closed his eyes. He drew in a long, deep breath. He was holding it and ready to relax when Harold and CeeCee came back into the office.

"CeeCee said you got a call from a lawyer. Who is it?"

"J.T. Weiss." Daniel said. He studied his Dad's face for a reaction. Harold would have been a great poker player, he thought, when the chips were down, Harold never showed his feelings.

"Holy smo…" Harold's voice trailed off. "Weiss has been called everything from a wacko to a wizard. Gary was able to get him for you?"

Before he could answer, his phone rang again. It was Gary.

"How did it go with Weiss?" he asked.

"Wow, I knew you had connections, but Weiss? For a moment I thought he was kidding," Daniel replied. "I'm still in shock. That guy has quite the reputation."

"There is a reason he does. Some people don't think he's aggressive enough. Believe me, he has an incredible ability to sift through all the minutiae and discover things that most people miss. He may drive you nuts with all the questions and his little observations, but I think you will like the outcome. That's what's important. I've got a meeting in a few minutes, but call me any time you need anything. You're not alone in this. I hope your meeting this afternoon goes well. Take care my friend." Gary hung up.

Bonus Stuff: Coaching has exploded in popularity in business. In this relationship, the coach helps the coachee separate the skills they have mastered from ones they need to work on or start learning. Where learning is required, a coach may either teach or point them in the right direction—books, courses, experts—to achieve the learning. Sometimes a coach will tell, instruct, or direct what needs to be done. Other times it is more about encouragement.

When we hear the term mentor we often mean someone separate from the job or even outside the company who can be a role model first and provide minimal coaching second. It is an honor to be a mentor as much as it is to have a mentor.

Those Lion Eyes by Will Bullas

15 BLURRY SECRET

Molly gripped the steering wheel so tight her knuckles were turning white. The security guard's words playing over and over in her mind. "I suggest you just get in and drive on like you said you would. I didn't see you here. I won't tell anyone you were here. Be safe, have a nice day."

She could swear she talked with someone named Angie, but no one seemed to believe her. Why did the guy at the gym act like everything was ok? She knew she wasn't eating right or sleeping well the past few days, but she was certain she wasn't losing her mind.

She came to the off ramp near the highway. There were several chain hotels, definitely out of her price range. She knew she shouldn't use her credit card. By now, she was sure someone was on her tail. She had already told the gym owner she was heading to Crandall. In case she was being followed, that was the last place she should go.

She pulled back onto the highway, she would have to drive until she found another small motel where she could pay with cash. "Calm down," she told herself. "You can think this through."

She dug into the side of the driver's seat for one of her books on tape. She pulled out the first disc she could get her hands on and popped it into the player. A woman's voice began to speak.

"How your brain tricks you - If you can't trust your own brain whose brain should you trust? The problem is that all our brains trick us into believing the wrong things at times. The extent of each of the tricks it plays are dependent in part on your thinking style. The other part is that your brain has developed protective measures and efficiency techniques that can lead it astray.

It recognizes and sees what it expects to see. Expectations are so strong an influence that it is not unusual for a person to insist they saw something that wasn't there or miss something that was there."

Molly bit at a fingernail and steadied the wheel with the other hand. "I know I talked to Angie, my mind can't be playing tricks on me." She turned up the volume and continued to listen.

"Your brain filters and perceptions color everything you see. From the time you were born your brain had to learn to filter out unimportant details and focus on important ones. However, what is important may change over time. Your filters may lead you astray by missing something you thought at one time was unimportant but now should attract your attention. Also, our brains believe that others must be seeing the world the same way.

The brain accepts the first solution to a problem. School taught you that there is one right solution. In business, once we think of a solution to a problem we might feel that we are done. But in business and in life in general, problems may have many potential solutions and the first one you think of may not turn out to be the best one. In fact, the first solution tends to be the most common one and certainly not the most innovative you can come up with."

Molly thought about Daniel and the many discussions they had about coming to a solution in different ways. She adored both Harold and Daniel and wished they could be more of a partnership, rather than the contentious father-son struggle that she witnessed regularly. Harold had experience to back him up, Daniel was always trying to be open to new ideas. Both men were right, but rarely agreed.

The woman on the tape went on, *"Once the brain makes up something it sounds like it must be true. After all, it is still sitting there in the brain to be retrieved as needed. Judgment may be based on a small amount of information or even misinformation but stated often enough, even if only thought, it becomes more real in our mind."*

"Angie was real, wasn't she?" Molly asked herself again. "Am I making her up? How could I?" She was lost in thought about the grocery store, the gym and the security guard when something struck her right front tire. She started to swerve and skid over the road.

"Correct slowly, turn into the skid," she heard herself say. She regained control and pulled off on the shoulder to collect her thoughts. She looked in the rear view mirror to see what she hit, but there was nothing there. Was it an animal? A pothole? She swept the hair off her face and buried her head in her hands for a moment. "I'm losing it."

She heard the sound of a car slowing and tires crunching across the gravel. Looking up, she saw a man in a dark sedan pulling up behind her. He didn't look like a policeman, there were no markings on the car. Her heart jumped. They found her, it surely had to be someone tailing her from the company.

"Miss, do you have car trouble?" the man was leaning down toward her passenger window while other cars whizzed by on the interstate.

"No, thanks. Just had to stop for a second," she said through the closed window. She motioned for him to go back. The man squinted one eye and looked at the odd assortment of clothing, groceries and books piled in the front seat.

"Are you on a trip?" he asked.

"Just a couple days away. I'm going to get started, I'm ok, really I am." She put the car in drive, but the man kept his hands on the car.

"It's not safe for a young woman to be traveling on her own."

"Gotta go," Molly revved the engine and pulled away, the surprised man standing in the wake of her dust.

Speeding away, she kept her eye on the man on the side of the road. She didn't have any idea who all worked for security at Wilson-Shaw, but now she was convinced they were looking for her. She thought about putting the battery back in her cell phone just to see who had sent messages, but she knew whoever did would get notification that she read the message. She had to leave the phone off and the battery out of it in order to stay off the radar.

She thought about what Daniel would say, there was no way to explain it to him. She couldn't change her mind now, she had been gone too long, the word was already out. Melanie played her part, now they were both beyond the point of no return.

She didn't want to think about thinking anymore, she decided to listen to music instead. She turned up the volume and started to reach for the dial when the woman continued, *"It treats risk as something to avoid or, for some people, something that adds excitement to life, like playing blackjack or driving too fast.*

It makes assumptions. You may be remembering the warning about what an assumption does to you and me, but that doesn't stop our brain. Our brain has learned that without assumptions we would have to wait until we collected 100% of applicable data for every decision. That isn't feasible. What is feasible is recognizing whenever we make an assumption so we can admit and be ready to reconsider when new information becomes available."

She snapped off the CD. She looked down at the speedometer, she was doing 85. She backed off the accelerator, the last thing she needed was a speeding ticket. A sign for the next exit listed only one motel, The Jeffersonian. She swerved into the right lane and drove up the ramp. A lone gas station sat atop the hill. There was a small sign pointing the way to the Jeffersonian, five miles south. Perfect, completely out of the way.

Molly ran through the options in her mind. If the Jeffersonian was a small mom and pop place, she could hide out in the back, pay cash and buy a little more time before anyone found her. She grew more hopeful as the road changed from four lanes to two. She assessed the amenities as she drove through the sleepy little town. A volunteer fire station, a small post office, two gas stations, one with fresh hot pizza, and finally, The Jeffersonian.

She pulled her car into the dusty lot and left it idling while she looked around. There were only two other cars in the lot. A station wagon with Utah plates, and a beat up pick-up truck with a license plate so wrinkled it was missing the state. It was almost 10 in the morning, so if there were more overnight guests, chances were they were on their way by now.

She turned off the engine and dug through her rumpled pile of clothes on the seat until she felt her wallet underneath. She checked herself in the mirror, ran her fingers through her hair and got out of the car. The midday sun was warm on her face.

The lobby was small, but neat. Molly hoped that was the case with the rooms too. She could hear a television playing in the background. She looked around to see if there was anyone near. There was no bell to ring or note on the counter. She could feel her heartbeat quicken, maybe she shouldn't have stopped. What if the man on the side of the road caught up with her and followed her here? What if they know where she is? She was ready to run back to her car when she heard a woman's voice. "I'm sorry to keep you waiting dear, do you need a room?"

The woman was short and round, with sparkling blue eyes. They reminded her of her grandmother. Molly relaxed a bit. "Yes, yes I do. I was hoping I could pay with cash. I have a credit card, but I'd rather not use it."

The woman studied Molly's face. "Of course dear. It's $39 a night. If you are paying cash, it's $35."

Molly dug out two twenty dollar bills. "I'll start with one night, it may be two, is that all right?"

The woman nodded and handed Molly a room key. Take number 11, it's around back. You can park your car between the dumpster and the white van. No one can see your car there, and the trash truck has already come by for the week.

Molly took the key and hesitated for a minute. "Don't I need to fill out something?"

The woman shook her head. "It's fine, $35 cash, one night, maybe two. That's all I need to know."

Molly drove around behind the motel and parked her car just where the woman suggested, tucked tidily out of sight. Maybe she thinks I'm running away from my abusive husband or something, Molly thought. Whatever she thinks, this works for now.

Molly wadded up the contents from the front seat under one arm and opened the door to the room. It was like stepping back into the 50's. A worn chenille bedspread, a small TV with rabbit ears and yellowed curtains, but everything was neat and clean. Molly shook out her clothes and hung up her shirts, smoothed out her jeans and laid them over the back of the chair.

She sat down on the edge of the bed. It was like settling into a soft, fluffy nest. She eased back on the bed and closed her eyes.

Bonus Stuff: There are different learning styles.
- Some people learn well from listening, they are auditory learners.
- Others learn better from what they see or read, they are visual learners. They will grab a piece of paper or paper napkin in a restaurant to draw their explanation.
- Kinesthetic learners learn best when they actually go through a trial process rather than just hearing or seeing a set of instructions.

For many, having access to all three methods deepens understanding.

16 BETTER STRATEGY

Daniel needed to run or get moving with something. The waiting was making him more anxious than ever. CeeCee ordered in lunch and was cancelling her afternoon appointment so she could stay with Daniel. Having her with him was calming, he remembered the early days when they were each other's biggest supporter.

He scrolled back through his phone to see if there were any messages from Molly that sounded unusual, but didn't see anything. The messages he had sent since she disappeared all showed as unread. He pulled out his tablet and was able to access some company emails. At least he was able to see everything that he had sent. He knew he shouldn't delete anything at this point, it would only make him appear guilty. He read carefully over every email concerning Molly. There wasn't anything about taking time off in any of them.

Brooke brought in the lunch order. Daniel and CeeCee ate in silence, while Harold paced the floor, leaving frantic voice mails for the board members.

"Everyone is ignoring my calls," he said in exasperation.

Daniel couldn't taste his food, it was bitter and heavy in his mouth. He couldn't believe how quickly the events of the day had shifted. He saw a shadow move across the floor. There in the doorway was a small, wiry man with waves of sandy hair over his collar and shoulders. J.T. Weiss was nothing like Daniel pictured. While the Weiss name was famous, he wasn't one for television sound bites and public appearances.

They shook hands, then Weiss set his briefcase on the polished conference table and pulled out a legal pad. "Daniel, I've notified the board to hold off on the vote until we can answer to the alleged charges. We need to begin with a frank discussion," Weiss looked at CeeCee and Harold. They both quickly gathered up their things and left.

"Let me start by explaining my technique with you. I've been accused of being too quiet at times. People equate action with noise, however, I believe there is a lot to be said for waiting for the other person to incriminate themselves. It's not underhanded, just an understanding of human nature. People are quick to blurt things out, because the silence makes them uncomfortable. They do most of the work for me. That's not to say I won't be thorough with you." His voice was clear and strong. Daniel relaxed.

"In that same manner, I purposely pause before I speak. That also makes people uncomfortable, but I like to think of it as avoiding foot-in-mouth disease," he chuckled. "I believe the pause is the most powerful part of speech in every language. It gives us a moment to think, it also gives the other person a moment to think, and they usually speak before you do. Comedians use the pause as part of jokes. Professional speakers for emphasis. And your brain can use it for all those purposes plus keep you out of trouble. I'm sure you've seen it in action; in sales he who speaks first gives the other person the upper hand." Weiss looked at Daniel.

Daniel deliberately waited before slowly nodding in agreement. Weiss laughed out loud. "I see we are already on the same page Mr. Shaw. I think this will be a productive, collaborative meeting."

Weiss listened intently while Daniel summarized the events of the past few days. At times, Weiss' silence made him uneasy, but he remembered what he said about incriminating yourself because you don't like the silence. Every so often, Weiss would repeat something Daniel said. It was starting to unnerve him.

"Mr. Shaw, let me stop you for a moment and let's clear something up," Weiss said. "I am not paraphrasing to make you uncomfortable. I am doing it to ensure that I understand what you are saying. Paraphrasing means summarizing what someone else said in your own words. To summarize, you have to understand, not just hear, the words. To do it effectively it must be shorter—a summary of the most important points, skipping the non-essential details.

Second, it has to be in your own words, not just a repeat of the words the other person used. If you were speaking in a foreign language, you could have a very different idea in your head of what the words meant. Your industry, the pharmaceutical industry, will have terms and code words that someone in the construction industry or manufacturing industry wouldn't understand. Yet if you were talking with them about a common issue, such as order fulfillment or budget concerns, they could understand you more clearly by interpreting with their own words. They can respond and correct or question what you said until it becomes clear you are understanding each other."

Daniel nodded. "I understand that, but how does that relate to responding to the board?"

"It always relates, regardless of who you are talking with. Do you listen well? Have you ever been accused of not listening? Perhaps you have a spouse or family member who has accused you of not really listening. It happens in business all the time, a person's mind wanders and they are no longer listening."

Daniel's cheeks flushed. It was one of the issues he and CeeCee seemed to argue about. He would be so tired when he came home in the evenings that he didn't actively listen to her or the kids.

"You may have seen a small child grab someone's face and turn it towards them to get full attention on what they have to say. A young child can get away with that. An adult, especially an adult in a business setting, cannot get away with it but I'm sure there are times when you wished you could.

Not really hearing what was said has negative repercussions. If you are at fault for not listening you may have to ask someone to repeat what they said. That is the same as admitting you weren't listening. You may answer the question you think they asked rather than the one they did ask. Before you are questioned by the board members, we need to be in agreement on the importance of active listening and that you can stay focused."

Daniel nodded.

Weiss continued, "Forcing ourselves to pay attention completely isn't easy. It has to be deliberate. If you know someone who listens well you may be aware how much people appreciate it. Feeling listened to feels good.

The best way to teach yourself to listen well is to get into the habit of paraphrasing after someone tells you something. This works well in meetings by paraphrasing the various contributions or decisions made. Knowing you will be paraphrasing helps you focus and pick up the most important elements so you are ready to speak. It forces you to think about what they are saying instead of dwelling in your own mind constructing what you want to say."

Again, Daniel deliberately waited with his response. "What I hear you saying is that regardless of what the board is asking me, I should listen to the question, paraphrase what I believe the question was and pause before I answer?"

"Excellent Mr. Shaw." Weiss started writing a few notes. Daniel began to fidget, he realized the power of the silence working in the room. He wanted to say something, anything. Then he took a deep breath and relaxed again. Weiss was making his point.

Weiss looked up from his notes and smiled. "You are a quick student. With some more practice you'll get comfortable holding longer pauses. Even if you are pausing because you don't know the answer, it is a sign of intelligence to hold your tongue instead of blurting out something wrong or silly you later regret."

"So there is no such thing as pausing too long?" Daniel asked.

"What do you think? Weiss asked. "Imagine for a moment that you could be watching yourself during one of those tough conversations you have had in the past. You are ready to say something you think clever or stinging, and your brain tells you to pause and think of the consequences. Might that change what you say? Might it change history? Might it change your future?

There are some things I said that I wish I could take back. There are some things I did that I wish I could do over. How about you?"

"Absolutely." Daniel stated. "I'm beginning to understand how powerful this strategy is. Yet I feel like you are counseling me, rather than finding out my side of things."

"We are establishing a mutual understanding, a foundation of common language and tactics. While I am representing you, I don't want there to be any doubt of my methods or competency. You are retaining me to defend you, you need to believe in me. If I can't establish that with you, how can I establish belief and credibility as your representative in sensitive matters?" Weiss asked.

"Then I would like to ask that you indulge me for a moment and tell me about your background. Not your schooling, that is all available on the internet. Tell me how you came to develop your operating standards, your strategies. It seems that these are a bit different than what I think they teach in law school." Daniel felt it was a fair question.

"Mr. Shaw, I'd be happy to and I think it directly pertains to our relationship. What you should know about me is that I am a keen student of how our brain works. In fact, I am fascinated by how it works when we are under stress, such as you are now. The brain can be easily fooled. Nowhere is that more obvious than when laws are broken or people act out against another.

Perceptions cloud our thinking. Until we are ready to be open to the possibility that our perceptions are keeping us from seeing the truth, the reality, the actual picture, we trust them. Just look at someone who believes they are in the right, even though they broke the law.

All prior learning and experiences determine how we see today, and what we think we see may not be the complete or correct picture. Our brains and our prior learning helps us focus on what is important to us. In fact, it has already decided what is important and what isn't. We need these shortcuts. We need to be able to focus, otherwise we get distracted by everything in our line of sight, range of hearing, field of touch and noticeable odor.

Information coming into the brain from any of our senses is not received passively or naively. Our brain filters and interprets based on past experiences and knowledge, even preferences. Our mind-set and our expectations control what the brain pays attention to. We need this process to function effectively and efficiently day to day. Yet we are missing a lot, and at times need to remind ourselves to open our mind to view the world more naively and see what shows up."

"Exactly how would you suggest changing that?" Daniel asked.

"There are ways to trick our brain into being more open and naive. Look at a picture upside down. Read a sentence backwards word by word. Close your eyes when you want to listen to sounds without pre-conceived notions. Do you ever watch that TV show that looks for musical talent where the judges have to listen with their backs turned to the musicians? Race, attractiveness, and other attributes are no longer considerations. Sometimes I wish jury trials were conducted that way," Weiss said.

Daniel nodded as he stared off into the distance. How often did he hold the silence, to mull things over, think of options, alternatives, and even consequences? He wanted to think he did it all the time, but in the case with Molly, he assumed everything was ok and didn't think over all the alternatives and consequences.

"I do still have one major problem." Daniel said. Weiss raised an eyebrow. "I have an assistant missing and allegations that she leaked industry information. My assistant Molly is the sister of the actress Melanie Meyers. The IT and Security departments have been tracking her but the trail has gone cold. Maybe I can't even say they are my departments now. What else can I do to find her? She is my only confirmation that I am not guilty."

"I believe you'll find our mutual friend Gary Brownlee to be a wealth of resources." Weiss said coolly. "I think we've covered enough for now. Get a bead on your missing assistant. I don't care if she's running away from a boyfriend or joined the circus. She needs to be back here, in the flesh and ready to answer questions."

Daniel grasped Weiss' hand and shook it firmly. "Understood."

Brooke was standing at the door as Weiss strode away.

"I'm sorry I wasn't at my desk when he arrived. Who is he?" she asked.

"He's my new counsel. J.T. Weiss. Now, I may be locked out of my email, but I am still CEO. I need you in here with a notepad and your phone. We've got some calls to make." Daniel ordered.

Daniel dialed Gary's number while Brooke sent Molly another text message. Gary didn't answer. Daniel tried to calm himself by taking another deep breath. He liked Weiss, even if he was a bit unusual. Brooke studied Daniel's face. "What are you thinking?" she asked.

"I'm thinking back over the conversations with Molly. I'm trying to remember anything she might have said about being in a bind, in trouble, money problems—but there's nothing. When she was here at work, she was extremely focused. Even when she wasn't working, she was always reading stuff about being more creative and productive. That reminds me—she always made notes in her planner, every phone call, every meeting. Is it still in her desk?"

They sprung from their chairs and raced to Molly's desk. Brooke and Daniel rifled through the desk. "I looked for her notes when I first filled in up here. I couldn't find anything other than some of her files. I couldn't find a notebook or anything."

"Did IT get into her email?" Daniel asked.

"I think so, Brad was handling that."

Daniel stopped. "Why was Brad taking the lead on this? Molly is in my department, it should have been handled here." He circled the desk. "Molly and Brad never interact in daily business here. I've never picked up on any friendship between the two. So why was he suddenly so interested in finding her? Daniel thought out loud. "Who was the first person in my office the day Melanie Meyers was on TV? Brad!"

"Wasn't he concerned about the value of the company?" asked Brooke.

"Yes, but why would he know about the TV story so quickly and make that connection? Who ran up here that day and turned the TV on? Craig—his whipping boy. I know they have a TV on for the stock values, but why would they know the Hollywood Minute was on right then?"

"What are you thinking?" Brooked asked.

"I'm thinking I need to pay a visit to Finance. Brooke, please go through Molly's desk with a fine toothed comb. Look for anything that may connect her to Brad, a phone number, a note, anything. We need to find her planner. I know you've been using her desk, but please, look everywhere you can think of." Brad hurried out of his office and down the hall to see Brad.

Brad's assistant was sitting at her desk. "Hello Mr. Shaw, can I help you?" she asked with a nervous smile. He walked around her desk toward Brad's closed office door. "I'm sorry, he isn't in. He stepped out earlier, he said he had a board meeting to prepare for this afternoon."

Daniel stopped short. He dropped his head and remembered—the pause. "I'm sorry, I got ahead of myself. I heard you say he was preparing for a board meeting this afternoon?"

"Yes sir. I didn't see it on the schedule, but he said it had been set a week ago." She answered.

"The board meeting was set a week ago?" Daniel asked.

"That's what he said to me. I remember saying that it wasn't on the calendar, but he said of course it was, it was scheduled last week." Her eyes were wide. "I'm sorry Mr. Shaw, I guess it wasn't on your calendar either."

"No, no it wasn't," Daniel ran his hand through his hair. He closed his eyes and thought for a moment. What am I missing here? He wondered. It's easy to jump to conclusions, but I need to think of several possible scenarios. He looked back at Brad's assistant and smiled. "Please call my office the minute he comes back," he asked.

"Don't you want to try to reach his cell?" she asked.

"No, I need to know when he is back at his desk." Daniel walked out of Brad's office.

Brooke was still going through Molly's desk as he returned. "Look at this!" She lifted up the desk calendar to find the previous months folded neatly and stacked in order. "She kept every month. I didn't read over much, but she has notes on there. Phone calls, people who stopped in, and a few doodles that I can't make out."

Daniel took the sheets and went to his desk. "Great work Brooke, I'll look these over." He opened the oversized sheets and scanned the first one. He recognized the doodles—they were mind maps of the various topics they talked about—workflow, press releases, publicity, and marketing. He tossed it aside and went through several more. Last October was on the bottom of the stack. There in red and blue ink was a diagram in the margin with the heading: Business| Brains |B.S

Bonus Stuff: Get comfortable using the pause to think or show respect while the other person speaks. Only on radio or an audio recording is a pause truly difficult because it will seem as if there is a technical problem. Any other time, body language can show patience or thoughtfulness.

.

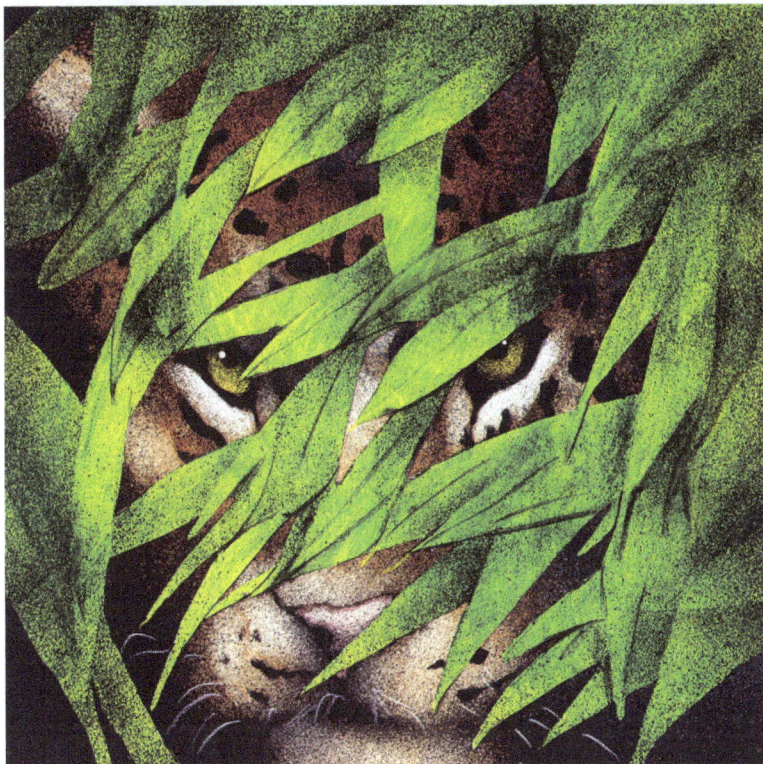

Beyond the Forest Green by Will Bullas

17 BURNING SUN

Molly woke with a start to a pounding noise outside. For a moment she couldn't remember where she was or how she got here. She heard it again and crouched by the window. Peering through the curtain she saw a man working on the gate on the trash dumpster enclosure. She looked over at her car—undisturbed. He hammered again and swung the gate closed. She held her breath while he fidgeted with the lock.

Molly shrunk down to the floor. The late afternoon sun cast a warm slice of light across the worn carpeting. She realized she had been asleep all day. She shook off the grogginess and raised up again to look through the curtains. The man had gone. Perhaps he was a real repairman after all.

She heaved herself up off the floor and went into the tiny bathroom. Splashing water on her face, she noticed her pale, tired appearance in the mirror. She thought about Angie, the drive, the man on the side of the road, the woman at the desk. "Are you losing your mind? Are you sure you want to go through with this?" she asked the reflection. "I'll tell you what, you are past the point of no return, so don't look at me like that." She turned away.

The silence in the room only made her edgier. She punched at the old TV set, a white spot appeared in the middle of the screen, she waited for a picture to appear, nothing. She pounded the side and the volume blared. "We'll be back with our exclusive report on a story we first brought you regarding up and coming star Melanie Meyer's brave battle with a mysterious disease."

Molly plopped down on the bed and stared at the set. After an endless parade of commercials, the story began. "Meyers, who announced that she was part of an FDA approved drug trial has had a dramatic decline in her health since her statement about the success of taking the drug RQ246, manufactured by Wilson-Shaw, a small pharmaceutical manufacturer. Today, Meyers was admitted to a local hospital which listed her in critical condition."

Molly gasped. "Critical condition? That can't be!" she yelled at the set.

The reporter continued, "This announcement sent shockwaves throughout the pharmaceutical industry. Stock values of Wilson-Shaw dipped again and there is a rumored call for removal of Daniel Shaw as CEO has been rumored."

"No, no," Molly jumped up. She dumped her bag on the bed and combed through the clutter for her phone and battery. She gathered them up and began to push the battery back into the phone, only to have it pop right back out. She stopped and took a deep breath. "Ok, calm down. Let's think this through," she said out loud. "If this is true, and Melanie is really sick, I can't reach her anyway. If I use my cell, then they will find me. I'm screwed. I'm sticking to the plan. But are they?"

Molly went back to the window and looked over the parking lot. It was quiet and empty. She eased the door open, still no one to be seen. She slipped out and headed for the front desk. Rounding the corner, she hesitated before walking to the front. Only a handful of cars were on the street.

"Are you ok?" the woman's voice came from behind her. Molly spun around.

"Yes, just fell asleep for a while, I'm not quite awake. I was hoping there was a pay phone around," she said.

"Oh honey, the only pay phone around is at the gas station, and half the time the cord is yanked out. If you need to make a call, use the desk phone," the woman smiled.

"It's long distance, I don't want to impose," Molly replied.

"No problem, I get free long distance with my internet." The woman leaned closer. "It won't show where you are calling from."

Molly scowled. "How does that work?"

"Well, it's just one of those rock-bottom phone services. Sometimes we have guests that need to call someone but not let them know where they are. You know, people in trouble, women mostly, who need to get somewhere safe."

Molly shook her head. "Oh no, I'm fine. Just taking a few days off work." Then realized she should have played into the scenario. Battered woman on the run. Darn it, she thought. I could have used that as a cover.

"Of course," the woman nodded. "Come with me."

Molly followed her into the office. The woman pulled the dingy rotary phone out of the file drawer. "It's ok, it really is safe." She nodded and then left the room.

Molly looked down at the phone. A hot, searing memory washed over her; her grandmother's kitchen, she and her sister rolling out cookie dough on the counter, the jangling bell on the bulky beige phone, and her grandmother's muffled cries. It was the call that changed everyone's lives. Molly's parents were dead. She shook off the movie playing in her mind, picked up the receiver, and dialed. The line was ringing on the other end, but it sounded odd. She dropped the receiver back in the cradle. She looked around for the desk clerk. No sign of her. She dialed again, a recording came on. "Hi, it's Mel. You know what to do at the beep!"

"Are you ok?" Molly whispered into the phone. "What's going on? I'm not using my cell, it's too risky, but I'm ok, on the move, and laying low. This has to be over soon."

The phone clicked again, "Hello? Molly are you there?"

"Yes, oh thank God. I was afraid you were in the hospital. I couldn't stay out of touch. What's going on?" she asked.

"Molly, I am in the hospital. My white cells are bottoming out, it has nothing to do with the drug, just bad timing, or maybe good timing depending on what happens. I had no clue your boss would be hung out to dry like that. That wasn't part of the plan, was it?"

"No. I would never have agreed to oust Daniel. I don't want to alarm you, but I'm afraid I am being followed, so I'm hopping around to little out of the way places. I can't talk long since I'm not sure this phone is safe." Molly said.

"It showed up as unknown on my cell. If you can get here, I'd love to see you, but I know it's a stretch."

"What hospital?" Molly asked.

"I'm back home, at Brentwood. Brock and I are back in touch, he's been here with me through this."

The news shocked Molly. Brock was her ex-brother-in-law and Fred Hirsch's son. "How much does he know?" Molly pleaded.

"He..." her voice cut out. "Oh my gosh Molly, he's calling."

"Brock?" Molly asked.

"No Him. HIM! Brad!"

"Whatever you do, don't tell him you've talked to me," Molly insisted. She heard the bell, then voices at the front desk. "I've gotta go, I'll try to get there as soon as I can."

"No, wait on the line, I'll get rid of him and then we can talk more, please Molly, just hang on!"

Molly could hear the conversation at the front desk through the thin panel door. She hoped they hadn't heard her talking on the phone. She leaned back to get a glimpse through the crack in the door. Two men were talking to the woman at the desk. She was shaking her head no. They began to turn away when one of them looked back at the door. Molly shrunk back. She gently placed the receiver back and held her breath.

"Good luck!" the woman called after them. She stood at the desk and continued sorting papers for a few minutes. Molly could hear the crunch of tires in the gravel lot as the car pulled away. Finally, the woman came into the office.

"They are moving on," she smiled. "You should be fine here tonight."

Dumbfounded, Molly nodded her head. "I'm sorry, I panicked and hung up on the call, is it all right if I call back one more time?"

"Of course. You don't have to tell me what kind of trouble you are in. In fact, the less I know, the better. I don't get tangled up in anyone's business. I just provide a warm bed and a safe place for the night. I don't provide bail money, counseling or therapy," she laughed.

"Thank you," Molly said. "By the way, I didn't catch your name."

"Angie," she smiled.

"You're kidding," Molly let out a nervous giggle. The woman winked and walked away. Molly picked up the phone and dialed again. It was answered on the first ring.

"Molly? Molly, listen carefully. They are looking for you. They've tried to trace your cell phone and credit cards. What are you doing for money? Where is your phone?"

"Calm down. I've already prepared for all of that. I'm staying in little cheap out of the way places, and I took the battery out of my phone so there wouldn't be a signal. Did he say he was looking for me himself? I could swear he almost found me in St. Mornay." Molly whispered. She wasn't convinced the woman wasn't listening.

"That's where they think you are. Don't go back that way, and as much as I hate to say it, don't come up here to see me right now either. He said he knows where I am."

"I can still get up there to see you," Molly insisted. "I'll figure out something. In the meantime, I'll check in with you when I can."

Molly hung up. She was tired of hiding. She wanted to call Daniel and let him know where she was. She wanted to go see her sister in the hospital and not be afraid. She picked up the phone and began to dial the office number. Not yet, she sighed and hung up.

Angie was mopping the entryway, humming to herself.

"Excuse me," Molly said. Angie stood up and smiled. "I know this is going to sound weird, but I've encountered the name Angie a couple times lately. I'm not sure how to explain this, but every time I heard it, things just seem to fall into place."

The woman leaned close. "You mean you don't know?"

Molly shook her head.

"Years ago there was a young woman on the run from an abusive husband. He had done unspeakable things to her. She left one night without money, a decent car or a place to stay. He found her just a few miles away, the beating was…" her voice trailed off. "After that, people around here formed our own silent network. Helping anyone else that was in danger or homeless. Whether you need a meal, a place to stay, or a safe way to make a phone call, Angie is a safe word, or code."

Molly thought back to the checker at the grocery. "Tell them Angie sent you," the security guard, "I won't tell anyone I saw you," it all made sense.

Molly squeezed Angie's arm. "I'm not running from a boyfriend, just a thing at my job. But thank you, thank you for all you do."

"I don't have to know, I just want to do what I can to help keep you safe," Angie hugged her tightly.

Back in her room, Molly sat on her bed and thumbed through her journal. She was not losing her mind, she thought. Things are falling into place after all. She just needed to stay with the plan. She flipped to the page with Business, Brains, and B.S. at the top. Her fingers traced over the words. "Brains will beat B.S." she said to herself.

She changed into a t-shirt and slipped between the covers. She wanted to get an early start in the morning.

Bonus Stuff: We make jokes about talking to ourselves, yet we often get a lot from having a conversation that allows us in a sense to step away and observe our own thoughts and reactions. There is no one better to ask penetrating questions, we feel safe in digging deep for answers. It is helpful to have been through a scenario in our mind before we have to describe or respond to it in a business situation.

18 BRAD'S SHENANIGANS

Daniel poured over the mysterious notations on Molly's October calendar. Under Brains there were arrows between various scribbles including DS and experiment. Under Business, there was board and value, and under B.S were the words, safety and debt payoff. He folded the calendar into a smaller square and tucked it into his jacket pocket just as Harold walked into his office.

"How did the meeting go?" Harold asked.

"That Weiss is a character, but I like him. He's all about strategy, focused thinking, deliberate processes." Daniel said calmly.

"He only bought you a little time though, the board is still going to meet."

Daniel nodded. "I'm going to meet with Gary and figure out what else I can do."

"You're not leaving the office are you?" Harold asked. "You should stay right here. You might not get back in the building if you leave."

"I agree." Harold and Daniel turned to see Brad standing at the door.

"What are you doing here?" Daniel demanded.

"We've just learned that Melanie Meyers has been admitted to the hospital in critical condition. Our stocks are plummeting. I've had several calls this afternoon from some of our biggest stockholders, they are calling for your head. Whatever stunt you pulled with that attorney to hold off the board meeting wasn't well received." Brad scolded.

Stop, breathe, remember the pause, Daniel told himself. He waited. Brad began to sway. "Well, Mr. CEO, what are you going to do?"

"I'm going to take a moment and review my options. If you'll excuse me, I need a moment with Harold." Daniel's voice was cool and smooth.

"I'm not sure you should be left alone," Brad argued.

"And it's your duty to guard me?" Daniel shot back.

"Brooke, call security and ask for two officers to come up here," Brad ordered.

Daniel smirked at Brad. "I don't recall naming you second in command here. Why don't you explain to me why you feel so compelled to take charge?"

"I…I'm not trying to take charge, but I believe it's imperative that we protect the company, and you…your fitness is in question. Someone needs to step up." Brad tripped over his words.

"Then the VP of Operations is next on the list," Harold said. "However, legal needs to be in on this and they are aware the vote has been tabled, therefore, it's not time to have anyone step up. Now, I believe Daniel made it clear he needs a moment, let's go." Harold opened his arms to guide Brad out of the office.

After Brad left, Daniel and Harold sat down together. "Son, what are you thinking?"

"Weiss said he was big on sitting back and giving others enough rope to hang themselves. I get the feeling that Brad has more interest in this than company value. It's almost like he's waiting for us to fail."

"How do you propose finding out?" Harold asked.

"We need to find out a bit more about him. I don't know much about his personal life, I always felt there was some sort of wall between us. Someone must know what he does, who he hangs out with. I've seen him a few times in the hallway talking on his cell phone, which I think is odd. Why would he need to sneak out of his office to use the phone?" Daniel wondered.

"Come to think of it, I came across him snarling into the phone to someone yesterday." Harold said. "He was worked up, but the moment he saw me, his whole demeanor changed. I didn't think much of it at the time, but now it makes me wonder."

Daniel picked up his cell and tapped at the screen. "Who are you...?" Harold asked. Daniel held up a finger.

"Danny boy, how are things?" Gary's voice carried through the phone speaker. Harold leaned back and relaxed. So far, Gary had been a game changer.

"Gary, I need some, ahem, research. Brad Davis, my CFO. The sooner the better."

Daniel hung up and looked at Harold. "I need to call CeeCee and the kids. Just to let them know what's up. I'll sleep here in the office tonight on the fold out. Why don't you go on home, relax. I think we'll have an interesting day tomorrow."

"Are you kidding? This is my company too, you are not facing this alone. I'll stay here and make some calls, I can do research too you know," he winked at Daniel.

Brooke knocked at the door. "This came for you." She laid a yellow, oversized envelope on the desk.

Daniel held it up toward Harold. "I wonder what good news this is," he quipped. He unlaced the flap and pulled out a sheet of company letterhead. "It's a formal notice for a deposition." He dropped the paper on top of his desk and looked out the window. "I suppose that at least gives me a fighting chance."

"That's great news," Harold said. "Call Weiss and let him know. If they depose you then you can set the record straight and we can get back to business."

Daniel spent the rest of the day pouring over his notebook. Looking over his parking lot lists, he chuckled at some of the things he worried about that now were trivial. He listed the kids and CeeCee as something he was worried about numerous times. He dialed CeeCee.

"Hi, are you at home?" he asked.

"Yes, I'm making dinner, will you be here?" she asked.

"No, Dad thinks I shouldn't leave, that they won't let me back in the building. I'll sleep on the pull-out here in my office. I just wanted to thank you for being here today. I know we've been off-kilter lately. There is a deposition tomorrow. That should clear things up and then we can get back to concentrating on us. The kids won't be in the house much longer and I think we should take a vacation. Something simple, like a cottage at the beach. It doesn't matter what we do, I just wanted to be sure you knew I still love you. I love our family. I'm sorry I lost sight of that for a while." The line was quiet. "Are you there honey?"

"Yes, yes I'm here Danny. Thank you, I love you too. If there is some way I can help you, don't hesitate. Good luck tomorrow."

That evening, Daniel and Harold shared takeout in the office. They talked about the past, the passing of Daniel's mother, the growth of the company, and how proud Grandpa Wilson would be. Daniel concentrated on Harold, listening and paraphrasing at times. He realized it was one of their best conversations, both men talking, listening and voicing opinions without the other interrupting or jumping to conclusions. They were both laughing over Daniel's first company presentation when his cell phone rang. It was Gary, Daniel put the call on speaker.

"Well Danny, it seems your Mr. Davis is a creative guy. He did a two year stint in Asia teaching English as a second language, mostly to corporate executives eager to do business in the U.S. Once he returned, he taught basic accounting and bookkeeping at the University. Again to foreign students."

"I guess that could be a little suspicious," Daniel replied.

"It gets better. He had a previous position at Smeltzer as head of accounting. Over the course of two years, the company had their first loss in over 40 years of business. He left the job and the losses reversed in a little over six months. I hate to say it, but I think he is cooking your books." Gary said.

Harold and Daniel nodded silently. "Anything else?" Harold asked.

"That's all I can find under the name Brad Davis. Perhaps you should pull his personnel file and see if any of this matches up. Now, I also have some information about Melanie Meyers, in case you need that," Gary added. "Miss Meyers was Mrs. Brock Hirsch. As in your previous employee Fred Hirsch; his son. The marriage ended shortly after Hirsch died in that hiking accident. Not sure that is a direct connection, but certainly interesting."

Daniel hung up and went to Molly's desk. He dug around in the top drawer, plucked out a set of keys and started toward the elevator.

"Where are you going?" Harold asked.

"It's best you don't know," Daniel asked.

"The hell it is. If you're going, I'm going." Harold hurried behind Daniel to the elevator.

The cleaning crew was working on the third floor as Harold and Daniel came out of the elevator. The men nodded and kept walking. As luck would have it, the door was open to the HR department. Daniel walked over to the wall of file folders and tried a drawer, locked. They waited for the cleaning lady to return to her cart in the hallway. Daniel opened the nearest desk and found a key ring neatly stowed in one of the top compartments. After several tries, he opened file drawer "D". Flipping through the files, he located Davis, Bradley J., gently closed the drawer, and pushed in the lock just as the cleaning lady returned.

"Excuse me, are you supposed to be in here?" she barked.

"Yes, I'm Brad Davis, Finance, just following up on some late paperwork." Daniel said. Harold studied the floor as they walked out while the cleaning lady shook her head and mumbled.

"Son, I hope that stunt was worth it," Harold said as they rode the elevator.

"Only one way to find out," Daniel said.

Daniel toweled off and unwrapped a shirt fresh from the cleaners. For the first time in years, he used the company gym and locker room. The run left him feeling recharged and more confident than he had in days. He was ready to face the day and the board. Weiss would be in his office within the hour and he was eager to hear more about Weiss' strategy and tactics.

Weiss arrived pulling a small wheeled crate full of books and papers. Daniel offered him coffee and joined him at the conference table.

"How are you feeling?" Weiss asked.

"Rested, oddly enough, and confident." Daniel replied.

The deposition was in four hours. Weiss pulled out a notepad and rolled his pen between his fingers. "Tell me about what you are doing that helps you grow as a company leader."

Daniel looked directly at him and waited a few seconds before answering. Weiss returned the stare. "You're asking what I do to improve my skills in leadership and management?" Daniel asked.

"Yes," Weiss smiled.

He began to recite the workshops, certifications and self-study materials he had used throughout the years. Weiss listened, only looking away to make notes. "Just in the past couple weeks, I received an invitation to the Trident Think Tank. I submitted my application, but this Melanie Meyers ordeal has overshadowed everything." Daniel sighed.

"I know the Trident program, I know it very well," Weiss replied.

"The invitation surprised me. It came at a time where I was doubting my ability to run the company."

"How so?" Weiss asked.

"My direct reports are very skilled, and they are great at implementing company initiatives. I feel I've done a lot to improve the creative, collaborative process, RQ246 being a result of that. But when it looked as if the drug trial was compromised, I panicked, I thought perhaps I had missed something. Then there was the working relationship with Harold. I perceived a lot of pushback from him when I tried to move us ahead. I would doubt myself and my decisions in light of his objections. He thought I should run the company the same way he did, while I was trying to bring more diverse thinking styles together."

"He seems to be on your side now," Weiss noted.

"It looks that way. Our conversations have improved through this. Something you said yesterday, about listening and paraphrasing hit home for me. Last night we had one of our best conversations ever. It was refreshing, and also productive." Daniel smiled.

"Let's get back to the Trident program. What did you want to glean from that?" Weiss asked.

"Confirmation, perhaps. Many of the directors are my age or older. I sometimes felt that age would be a factor in managing them. That is the area where I lack confidence. I wanted to be sure that my efforts to shift the company culture were on target. I want to see Wilson-Shaw continue to develop new methodologies and products. I believe in what we do here, people's lives are positively impacted by our products. Lives are improved, and one day, I'd like to see us develop a drug that would eradicate disease. That has been the underlying passion for my grandfather and dad, and for me too. I want to ensure that passion is still alive and thriving throughout our company. Not only in the lab, but that everyone in the company understands their role is important to the overall product."

"Your passion is duly noted," Weiss said. "What about the actual policies you've created to make that happen?"

"I believe our working groups are evolving. One of the policies I introduced is to mix up the work group across departments for a diverse mix of input. Creative problem solving—I stress the importance of considering more than one solution, different ways to brainstorm, standing outdoors for quick meetings. That sort of thing."

"What about your hiring policy?" Weiss asked.

"I think we've made the change to hiring a better mix of people. I think one of the struggles that an established business has is doing it the way we've always done. That was one thing that Harold would say, 'We've only done it this way' and that ruffled me. Like putting different people together for work groups, looking for people with a strong sense of curiosity and openness gives us a creative advantage. New hires are coming from diverse backgrounds, ages and schooling."

Weiss nodded. "One more question. How can you lead your company to continue to learn and grow?"

"You mean if I'm not removed as CEO? Shouldn't that be our first concern?" Daniel asked.

"Indulge me, what would your answer be to the Trident interview?"

"I want to see Wilson-Shaw be a leader in collaborative excellence. Individuals work well with whatever team they are in, they have the skill to tap into various thought processes, and appreciate those with other experiences and thinking styles. From there, a solid company culture evolves that uses those techniques to interact with customers, vendors and other researchers outside our company. We think, create, problem solve, and grow holistically."

Weiss rolled the pen between his fingers. "Impressive."

"Thank you, but at the moment, I don't see that serving me well. The board has been reluctant to embrace the new ideas and styles I am trying to develop. I feel like this stock devaluation is just the excuse they have been waiting for to move me out." Daniel said.

"What about Mr. Davis? You mentioned he seemed to be leading the charge."

"Well, I've uncovered some background on Brad. I want to share it with you." Daniel leaned across the table.

For the next hour, Daniel and Weiss poured over Brad's personnel file and Daniel's notes. Finally, Weiss checked his watch and began to stretch. "You need to get out and get some fresh air, let's walk over to Radigan's for lunch."

The sun was warm on Daniel's face as they walked to the restaurant. He realized he had stayed sequestered in the office for over 24 hours. He started to ask Weiss another question about the proceedings coming up, when he was cut off. "Let's give that a break, give your mind a chance to rest. Let's talk about something else, baseball, your children, music." Weiss suggested.

They chose an outdoor table and waited for their order. Daniel sat back and watched people scurrying along the sidewalk, some on their phones while others kept their heads down, avoiding eye contact. A young woman in a bright yellow dress seemed to float down the sidewalk, smiling and saying hello to people. Weiss noticed him watching the parade of people going by. "Different is not better or worse," he said.

Daniel raised an eyebrow. "Why do you say that?"

"Everyone walking along is different. Some are keeping to themselves, others are talking on their phones, and then that girl, she is purposely trying to engage people to get them to react. It's the same way with our brains. People would call a genius different. At the opposite end of the spectrum, they would label someone with less intelligence different also.

Children are gifted in different ways and need to be encouraged to grow.

The child that asks too many questions is sometimes thwarted because an adult thinks they are annoying, but that is how that child learns.

It's amazing that at only three pounds, our brains have 86 billion neurons. So many people think they can't improve their brain power, but it is possible. It starts with paying attention to your own thinking. Being aware of how your brain learns, understands, stores, and recalls information."

Daniel nodded. "Yes, I've heard that at a workshop on that topic. I came away understanding that I tend to be one who feels their way. Like when I take time to run, keeping my body engaged allows my brain to wander, consider new ideas and solve problems."

"That's a great revelation," Weiss said. "Feeling is just one of the dimensions of thinking, we use them all, even though one may dominate over the others."

"I have the feeling you are going to explain the differences to me," Daniel chuckled.

Weiss nodded. "Imagine a circle divided into four quadrants, A, B, C & D. Quadrant A decision makers want to move fast. They want to get just enough information to point to a decision, decide, and move on."

"That's Harold for sure," Daniel said.

"Bs spend as much time as it takes, or they are allowed, to gather all the data to be sure before making a decision. Bs are concerned about the risk and embarrassment of making a wrong decision. Imagine after such care was taken that you bring your B quadrant business associate some new data that shows there should have been a different decision. Bs will defend their decision even in the face of conflicting information. You better have plenty of proof to get a B to change his mind.

Decision-making for Cs requires collecting the team's thoughts and preferences on the subject. The correct decision is the one that most on the team believe is correct. For them, decisions are team decisions and any changes go back to the team for discussion."

"I see that a lot in our research teams, they rely on team input heavily," Daniel said.

"Finally, the Ds, when confronted with the need to make a decision will look at the big picture, the larger goal, to dictate which way to decide. The details aren't important, or at least not as important as keeping focused on the big picture, the forest, not the individual trees."

"So what is the best way?" Daniel asked.

"They all have merit, it's understanding the different ways that is important. Those you put in charge of others need to have a full understanding of how to blend these styles in order to help your company culture match your vision." Weiss said.

"It takes time," Daniel said. "I see some change, but getting people to adopt a new perspective scares them. Some are afraid to speak up with new ideas. They are mired in past experiences where wild, new ideas were met with skepticism. It's like trying to turn around a battleship in a pond."

"That it is, but it shouldn't discourage you from making the effort. You're a smart man, Daniel. Have confidence in your ability, even when you question it. Everyone in positions of power should have a healthy dose of self-awareness. That person is a much better leader than one who is convinced they are never wrong."

Daniel's phone vibrated with the reminder alarm. "We need to get back. I have to tell you, I am nervous."

Weiss nodded his head. "Just remember the power of the pause, stay calm, and you'll have the most power in the room."

Bonus Stuff: Change can be difficult, but a company that stands still falls behind. Not everyone sees change as a positive. There may be people who drag their feet, deliberately, or maybe not deliberately, but subconsciously. Neither can be ignored.

19 BOARD SOLUTION

Muffled voices came from behind the glass walls of the board room. Seven men were already seated. A clerk with a recorder sat near the end of the table along with Vaughn from Legal.

Weiss looked at Daniel and nodded. "We'll be fine."

Daniel buttoned his jacket and entered the room. Two of the board members rose and extended their hands. Daniel shook them, said hello then looked directly at the others. He tried not to think he was already outnumbered.

The board president tapped his silver pen on his tablet. "It is 1 p.m. We'll begin." He cleared his throat and shifted forward in his seat.

"This board meeting is an informal investigation into the events relating to a leak of privileged information regarding our in-trial drug, RQ246 and its correlation to the dramatic devaluation of Wilson-Shaw stock. All board members are present, as well as counsel for Mr. Shaw and company counsel,

Vaughn Williams. It is our mutual desire to bring about clarity and understanding, is it not, Mr. Shaw?"

Daniel paused, then nodded. "Absolutely."

"Mr. Shaw, please state your name for the record, and have your counsel do the same," Vaughn began.

"Daniel Wilson Shaw"

"Jerome Taylor Weiss"

The other board members sprang to attention, the name Weiss commanded big money. It was a given that anyone that came up against him in court wouldn't have it easy. Vaughn studied the two of them, Daniel returned the gaze. Bring it on, he thought.

Molly had been on the road nearly four hours. For the first time in several days, she felt rested and confident. She had been listening to a CD and sorting out the events of the past week, realizing that fear and fatigue had clouded her thinking.

The woman on the CD continued, "You are being paid to think! In fact to think better, clearer, more logically, more critically, and more creatively. It's important to continually improve your thinking. Thinking more critically gives you more confidence in your decisions. Thinking more critically and being able to demonstrate it gives others more confidence in you. The result is better decisions, more self-confidence, and more respect at work."

"I've thought this through critically and completely," she said back to the CD. "I'm going to set things straight!" Molly fished the battery out of her bag, slid it back into the compartment and the phone powered on.

Vaughn read the summary of events reported to his office. It was apparent to Daniel that the bulk of his information was hearsay from Brad. Brad first alerted Vaughn about Melanie Meyers, then later suggested that Molly was related. Daniel listened carefully and made notes. The timeline didn't quite make sense. It seemed Vaughn knew about Molly's relationship and alerted Security and Legal well before he told Daniel.

Daniel scribbled a note on his legal pad and slid it in front of Weiss. He saw Weiss look down at the paper, then close his eyes. Daniel pulled the pad back.

Vaughn continued his summation. "As counsel for Wilson-Shaw Pharmaceuticals and this board I call for the removal of Daniel Wilson Shaw as CEO due to poor performance, failure to protect company information, and questionable personal relationships fostering the collusion to deliberately devalue the company for personal gain."

Daniel kept his composure and looked across the table at the board. Out of the corner of his eye, he could see Weiss' hand, smoothing out the table. *Pause.* They waited. The men across the table began to shift and squirm. Vaughn dabbed at his forehead with his handkerchief, while the board president poured a glass of water, took a small sip and cleared his throat. Daniel couldn't believe how quickly the façade was crumbling. These powerful men, all full of bluster, were coming unglued by the silence.

Finally, Weiss spoke up. "On the surface, it would seem these charges are valid. However, we are all familiar with times that we were convinced by data, circumstances or results. Since we had an answer, we decided we were done thinking about it. If you think there is only one answer—yours—then you have closed down your mind."

"What kind of horse hockey is that?" one of the board members blurted.

Weiss held up his hand and smiled. "Simply the truth about how our minds work. Once we have an answer, we think the issue or problem is solved. When in fact, there could be numerous answers. This is one of those instances. I humbly ask that you all suspend any pre-determined outcome for the sake of true discovery of the facts."

Vaughn coughed. "Mr. Weiss, I'm sure Mr. Wilson would appreciate you keeping your time short, after all, he is paying you by the hour."

Weiss smiled. "I will ensure my client has the best representation I can give him. Mr. Shaw and I thoroughly discussed this situation. I am confident in his ability to continue in his current position as CEO. I am also confident that he played no part whatsoever in the leak of industry information or misconduct with Molly Messersmith or Melanie Meyers."

"That's very well and good," Vaughn replied. "But we need concrete evidence to the fact. Mr. Shaw has some serious charges to answer to."

"Then fire away," Daniel said.

Vaughn and the board members lobbed question after question at Daniel. With Weiss sitting beside him, he felt calm and remembered to pause, repeat questions back, and take his time answering. It was playing out before him just as Weiss had predicted. The board members were uncomfortable with long pauses and silences. Daniel skillfully answered each charge, the board's attempt at trick questions flopped.

Brad was pacing the hallway outside the boardroom when his cell phone rang. A man from Security said they detected Molly's cell phone signal within 15 miles of the building. "That can't be," Brad said. "Can you pinpoint it any better than that? Get someone on her tail. Find her!" Just as he hung up, he felt someone behind him.

"Hello Brad, everything ok?" Harold asked.

"Yes, of course. I was just waiting to hear the outcome from the board vote."

"I'm sure they will take their time to hear all the facts. Daniel and his attorney are well prepared. It's interesting that you are so invested in the outcome." Harold said.

"I have several high profile stock holders to answer to, they want answers," Brad replied.

"As they should, you're doing a great job keeping them informed. You've had your finger on the pulse of this the entire time. I'm not sure anyone has told you what a great job you're doing," Harold smiled.

Brad looked sheepish. "Thank you. I suppose I should get back to the office."

Inside the board room, the temperature was warming up. As cool and collected as he appeared on the outside, Daniel felt the rivulets of sweat dripping down his back. The board had asked him the same question seven different ways, but his answers remained consistent. He had no direct knowledge or contact with Melanie Meyers. He did not know anyone in the company that was administering the drug trial and he had never had inappropriate contact with Molly.

Weiss noticed the temperature too and called for a brief recess. He and Daniel stayed behind as the board members left the room. "You are doing great. You've handled their repeated questions very well. It certainly gets them agitated when you take your time to answer. I'm sure they wanted to throw you out of here in less than 30 minutes. The fact that we've controlled the pace is in our favor."

Daniel got up and took a walk, stopping off in the men's room to splash cold water on his face. Harold was waiting outside the door when he came out. "How's it going son?"

"They are a tough crowd, it seemed most of them had already decided I was guilty before we walked in. With Weiss' coaching, I've been able to get them to consider that things are not as they seem. I hope it's enough."

Vaughn stood at the boardroom door, "Daniel, we're ready to reconvene." Daniel nodded and headed for the door as Vaughn's cell phone buzzed. Daniel noticed the startled expression on his face. "Excuse me, I need to take this call."

When Vaughn returned to the boardroom, his face was pale and sweaty. Daniel looked at Weiss, who merely shrugged.

"I have a few more questions, Mr. Shaw." Vaughn continued. "Is there anyone within this company in whom you have experienced a lack of confidence?"

Daniel looked at Weiss and smiled slightly. "I don't want to act on feelings or hunches. However, I am aware of some conflicting background on one of the company directors."

"Who?" one board member shot back. "This company will not tolerate fraud in any form."

"Our head of Finance and Accounting, Brad Davis, appears to have a spotty work history. The information in his personnel file differs from other research on him," Daniel paused. I've already opened the can of worms, here it goes, he thought. "Brad's file in HR lists his work history as a volunteer digging wells in Central America after graduating from college. However, he was teaching English as a second language to corporate executives in Asia. He also taught accounting and bookkeeping to foreign students here in the city before working at Smeltz for a few years. Neither of those positions are listed in his file. Instead, he listed positions at two manufacturing companies. Neither of those companies have any record of a Brad Davis working there."

Vaughn wiped his forehead again and looked down at his cell phone.

"So he has a creative work history, how does that relate to the problem we are in?" another board member asked.

"I believe we will have the answer to that," Vaughn said as he motioned to someone standing outside the door.

Daniel turned around and nearly collapsed. It was Molly.

"Ms. Messersmith, please come in and have a seat." Vaughn said. Molly's hair was disheveled and her clothes were wrinkled. It wasn't her usual crisp and professional attire. She eased into a chair opposite from Daniel. She smiled weakly then looked to Vaughn. "Let the record show that Ms. Molly Messersmith has joined the proceedings. Molly, please repeat to the board what you told me earlier on the phone."

Molly looked around the table. Her tongue caught in her throat like sandpaper. It was time to come clean, she only hoped it was the safe place to do so. She tried to form words, but failed. Daniel stood up, poured a glass of water and slowly pushed it across the table to Molly.

"I was approached by Brad Davis back in October," she began. "He said he discovered I had a sister who was an actress and that he needed someone to make a public statement for him. In exchange, he would pay us $50,000 each. I asked what kind of statement, and he said he just needed her to say something positive about RQ246 while on the red carpet."

Daniel couldn't believe what he was hearing. Several of the men began to talk over one another. Vaughn held up his hand. "Please continue."

"I said no right away," Molly added. "It was difficult, because I needed the money. I think that's why he first approached me. I was way behind on bills, I had been sending Melanie money out in Hollywood because she wasn't getting any acting gigs. $50,000 would solve a lot of problems." She looked at Daniel. "I said no, I knew it wasn't right."

Daniel nodded back. "Then why did you run?" he asked.

"Brad persisted. Then he started to scare me. He said that things happen; brake lines get cut, gas leaks and hiking accidents. I didn't ask him outright, but I knew he meant Fred Hirsch. See, he also knew that Fred's son was married to Melanie. He had approached Fred with the same deal right after Brock and Melanie got married. Fred said no too."

"Why on earth did Brad want a statement about RQ246?" Daniel asked.

"He wanted the company stock to shoot up. He acted like he was Melanie's agent, sending press releases, and coaching her on what to say."

"That makes sense," Daniel said. "The moment that was on TV, he was in my office. Acting as if it were terrible news."

"Then a few days later Melanie was supposed to say the drug had made her sick. But in fact, she has Lupus, it flared up and she had to go to the hospital. It was just a coincidence, but it played right into Brad's plan. Stockholders would bail and there would be a lot of cheap stock, he had Asian investors ready to jump in and take the majority share of Wilson-Shaw." Molly's eyes were red and teary. "I was supposed to show up to work just as if nothing was happening, but I panicked and left town."

Daniel let out a heavy sigh. "So did Melanie actually take any RQ246?" he asked.

"No, she was only supposed to say she did. Then when the press started calling he had the calls routed to him. He said he was her agent. He was the one who leaked the information about the drug still being in trials. I didn't know he was going to do that," she wailed.

"So to your knowledge, Melanie Meyers was not included in the drug trial?" Vaughn asked.

"I'm certain of it, she only heard from Brad on the phone, he never sent her anything. Not even the money." Molly straightened up and dabbed at her eyes. "He left both of us some frightening voice mails. At times, I was certain he was having me followed."

"Your cell phone signal was traced," Daniel said. "You and I were in St. Mornay at the same time, according to Security."

"Yes we were," Molly smiled. "I was in the booth across the bar from you when you had dinner with Gary Brownlee. I wanted to walk over and come clean right then, but I figured I was already screwed, so I slipped out the side door and took off."

"Miss Messersmith, did you have threats made against your life by Brad Davis?" Weiss asked. Molly nodded. "Please answer for the record," Weiss urged.

"Yes, I did." Molly said.

Vaughn slammed his notebook shut. "I recommend that security be notified to detain Mr. Davis and that we notify law enforcement. Miss Messersmith, you will need to file a police report. Are you willing to do so?"

Molly nodded. Daniel tried to catch her eye, but she kept looking away.

"I propose that Daniel Shaw retain his position of CEO and call this session adjourned," the board president said. The others murmured their agreement. As the men got up to leave, Vaughn was just outside the door dialing security when Brad approached the board room. Molly looked up and saw him looking directly at her.

Two of the board members gathered around Brad. He continued to glare at Molly. Daniel stood up, closed the door, and sat next to her.

"I'm so sorry, I should have told you right away. I'm so ashamed that I let him blackmail me that way. It wasn't about the money anymore, it was about protecting Melanie. I knew he had something to do with Fred's death. He kept talking about Fred's hiking accident, saying it wasn't an accident." Molly sniffed.

"You did the right thing, coming back here," Daniel smiled. "I found your notes on your calendar, it must have been the same time he approached you with the plan. You had Business, Brains, and B.S. written there. Care to explain?"

Molly smiled. "Well, you know me, I need to have a map for everything. I knew I had brains, and I tried to look at his plan as a business transaction. It was just an effort to be ok with the idea of providing a service, you know, an actress to play a part."

"But what was the B.S.?"

"Well, it stood for Brad's Scam, but as it turned out, it is just plain old B.S."

Bonus Stuff: Wisdom and Judgment
Data and knowledge can be researched by anyone in minutes. It takes wisdom and judgment to decide what to believe and what to do with the information.

20 EPILOGUE

A warm breeze blew across the patio carrying the tangy aroma of barbequed chicken. CeeCee gave Daniel a playful nudge as she carried a tray of drinks to the table. He looked around the yard. Harold had cornered Weiss and was peppering him with stories of the way Grandpa Wilson handled business. Molly, Melanie, and Brock sat near the pool, talking with Daniel's kids.

Molly looked over at Daniel and smiled. He nodded and gave her a thumbs up.

As they all gathered at the table, Daniel raised his glass. "I'm so happy to have all of you assembled around our table tonight. The Brad Davis trial was stressful, but now that he is behind bars for extortion and the murder of Fred Hirsch, we can move on. We had some dark days, but with some insight, logic and creative thinking, we have an outcome better than I think any of us expected. Everyone is safe, Wilson-Shaw is back on solid ground, and RQ246 is on track for release as planned. On a personal note, CeeCee and I are going away for a second honeymoon, and after that, I will reconsider my role at Wilson-Shaw."

Molly and Harold gasped. "What?"

"Don't worry, I am not leaving as CEO, but I want to explore more ways to bring in diversity in thinking styles, personalities and backgrounds. I want to give some serious study to the best way to achieve a culture that will lead the way in ground breaking research and new products. Hopefully, I will still make it into the Trident program and bring back even more innovative strategies." He said.

Weiss laughed. "Daniel, you were accepted the minute I took you on as a client."

"What do you mean?"

"I developed the Trident Think Tank with a man named Greg, whom I believe you met one day at a baseball game. He and Gary Brownlee called and said you were someone I should get to know. In preparing for the deposition, I learned a great deal about you. As I stated then, you are a sharp man, and you are more than capable. Have confidence in your ability, even when you question it. I see nothing but great things ahead for Wilson-Shaw and for Daniel Shaw."

Everyone around the table clinked their glasses. "Here, here!"

ABOUT THE AUTHOR

Hazel Wagner, PhD, MBA, CMC

Internationally acclaimed speaker, author, and seminar leader.

Hazel believes, speaks and writes about lifelong learning, curiosity, application of critical and creative thinking in tandem, genuine interest and skepticism to find answers and solutions, and most of all, open listening and questions.

Hazel Wagner has inspired audiences all over North America, Europe, and Asia. Her books and webinars reach even further. She has taught both mathematics and international marketing at the university level including Northwestern University, Kellogg Graduate School of Management, and DePaul University. She has turned math-phobics into math wizards, and at least two that she knows about into PhDs like herself. She has held sales and marketing positions in f100s and start-ups. She is an entrepreneur and a constant charity volunteer.

She writes books, blogs, and delivers keynotes and seminars around the world. Her other book, *Power Brainstorming, Great Ideas at Lightning Speed,* is available where ever good books are sold including online.

For more information or to have Hazel speak at one of your events contact her b9d, inc. office in Illinois or visit www.hazelwagner.com or www.brainstorming-that-works.com.

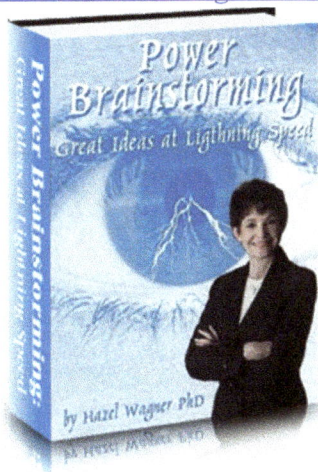

Praise for Business, Brains & B.S.

A superb book! Dr. Wagner provides a wonderful cross between reading a Tom Clancy novel and a Jack Canfield success guide!!! She challenges the conventional wisdom of how we think, both individually and as a group, and how we communicate and handle a crisis. She provides solid hands on techniques to create a more creative thought process while demonstrating concepts of communicating to a variety of audiences. The key with this book is the unique approach she takes in presenting a fictitious case study in a fast-paced mystery and suspense format that makes for an easy, entertaining and engaging read. It does this while providing valuable insights and lessons to learn. No business leader should be without a copy of this book in their library."

- Salvatore M. Capizzi, Executive Vice President, Chief Sales & Marketing Officer, Dunham & Associates Investment Counsel, Inc.

San Diego, CA

"Knowledge is not necessarily wisdom. This book makes that distinction and shows how to extract everyday wisdom from your experiences. Read it and reap."

- Sam Horn, author of POP! and Tongue Fu!

"This book will help you become a better manager. Period! But there's something more. "Business, Brains, and BS" is one hell of a good book! Ms. Wagner is every bit as good an author as she is a consultant, and this book is as good as most any "whodunit" you might choose to read this summer. Beach reading totally at home in the boardroom."

- William Matthies, Author, "The 7 Keys to Change"

For me it made reading a business book fun, I accidentally read the business book, while I was turning pages in the mystery. It read fast and the information stuck to my brain better when I forgot that I was learning something."

— *Keith C.P. Wagner, President, Fabrik Industries, Inc.*

"As anyone who has met me knows, I remind people to be outrageous, and that is how I would describe the title and style of Hazel Wagner's new book, Business, Brains and BS. She knows how to grab and keep your attention so that you emerge wiser.

- *Mikki Williams, CSP, CPAE, professional speaker/executive coach and producer of Speaker Schools*

www.ingramcontent.com/pod-product-compliance
Lightning Source LLC
Chambersburg PA
CBHW061744270326
41928CB00011B/2366